A Countryman's Journal

*Views of Life and Nature from
a Maine Coastal Farm*

A Countryman's Journal

Roy Barrette

Rand McNally & Company
Chicago • New York • San Francisco

Illustrations by Richard Gorski

Copyright © 1981 by Roy Barrette
All rights reserved
Printed in the United States of America

Library of Congress Cataloging in Publication Data
Barrette, Roy.
    A countryman's journal.

      1. Country life—Maine.   2. Barrette, Roy.
I. Title.
S521.5.M2B37   974.1'45   81-7367
ISBN 0-528-81110-X   AACR2

First printing, 1981

This book is dedicated in gratitude to my wife, but for whom I would never have lived in Maine; to Isabel Rector Russell, who inspired me and was able to read my script even when I was unable to do so myself; and to my good friends J. Russell Wiggins and Lawrence K. Miller, editors extraordinary, without whose interest these chronicles of a Maine countryman would never have escaped the pages of his personal journal.

Contents

Part Three   *What is this life, if full of care*
We have no time to stand and stare?

Part Four   *All times are his seasons*

A Countryman's Journal

Introduction

A hundred and twenty-five years ago a man whose name I do not know built a house on the crest of a small hill overlooking the lower reaches of Blue Hill Bay. He sited it so that in midsummer he could see the sun rise over the mountains of Mount Desert Island and in the winter, when it is farther south, watch it crimson the spruces on the smaller offshore islands.

While I have nothing with which to document my surmise but internal evidence (the layout of the barn, the stone walls, old foundations, field wells, and scraps of information gleaned here and there over a score of years), I believe he was more of a farmer than were most of the town's residents. When I bought the place, the then-current owner Roy Bowden and his wife were storekeepers in a small way. The real estate agent told me I could make "half a living" out of the store and gas pump in front of the barn. About all the farming then being done was when a crop of hay (if a scant growth of poverty grass and weeds could be dignified by that name) was taken off the back field. The owners were old and the last of their line and, after we had agreed on a figure for the place, were happy to accept, as a gift, the part of the building they were living in. They moved it to a new foundation a half-mile down the road and occupied it for fifteen more years, until they died.

When the man who built the house lived here I am sure that he, like most of his contemporaries in the village, took part of his living from the sea. It would have been especially easy for him because the land runs down to the bay. In 1852 he could have filled a pail with flounders on any incoming tide. Clams were on his shoreline for the digging (a few still are), and lobsters were so plentiful they were selling for $12 a ton. The bay was floored with scallops, and schools of mackerel fretted the water in summer. If he owned a boat—as almost everyone did and most still do today—he could have gone a little off shore into deeper water and loaded it with cod and hake and haddock whenever the weather was fitting.

The population was larger in his time than it is in mine. The town was self-contained and self-supporting. Roads were from poor to bad and almost impassable in "mud time." There were no inland towns in this part of Maine because travel was by water, and without access to it there was no convenient means of communication. Today the population is between 500 and 600; in 1850 it was 1,200, and all found employment in the town or nearby. There was work for everyone who wanted it, and as there was no unemployment insurance or other governmental inducement to remain idle, everyone who could work did. There were several boatyards (there are still two) where skilled craftsmen built anything from peapods to 300-ton schooners engaged in foreign trade. For the most part these vessels were owned by local people who, frequently, also sailed them. In 1876 there were ninety-five men out of a total of 260 voters who were masters of vessels of some kind. If you add to this figure the number who would have made up the crews, you arrive at a substantial portion of the town's male population.

Most of those who did not actually go to sea worked in related industries: the shipyards, the canneries, and the fish factories. It is recorded that in one year the town exported 30,000 gallons of fish oil, 25,000 boxes of smoked herring, and 500 tons of fish scrap, plus 350 tons of lobsters. Fish scrap brought $9 a ton—almost as much as lobsters.

The town covers 8,000 acres, but most of it is and always has been swamps, ledges, glacial moraine, and woods. The eight-acre field behind my house is one of the largest open fields in town. I suppose, at one time, it might have made a crop of potatoes (for I grow good ones now in my garden), and there are records of oats and barley being cultivated. In the big year before the potato blight of 1845, the town exported 10,000 bushels of potatoes, but that never happened again. While most people had a garden, grew their own vegetables, and kept a cow or a pig or two, there was little or no commercial farming. The size of the fields and barns on this place suggests that the first owner probably sold some produce locally, but he, like the rest of the villagers, would have been principally a subsistence farmer.

Most Maine coastal towns depended upon the sea for a living, and this one was no exception. When the Eastern Steamship Company hauled down its flag in 1935, it signaled the end of the town's Golden Age, though it had been going downhill for years. The internal combustion engine finally killed it, as it has so many other things. The automobile put the small steamboat companies out of business and then—aided by the airplane—the railroads. The only public transportation the town ever had was by water, so when the steamboats stopped running, the town gradually and quietly stopped breathing.

When my wife and I came here more than twenty years ago and bought the unknown builder's house and began to make it habitable (the part we kept had not been lived in for years and boasted neither heat, plumbing, water, nor electricity), the young wife of the man we employed to do the work told us it was the biggest thing that had happened in town since she was born. Though we were old enough to be her parents, it was also the biggest that had happened to us since we were born.

We did not come here to escape anything, but to find something. Our family was grown and married, we were healthy and reasonably well off, and I had skills that could be employed here as well as anywhere else, so we were free to do as we wished. What we desired was what a great many people seek in these latter days of the twentieth century, an opportunity to rediscover some of the virtues of a more stable, simpler society. While everything has not developed as we expected, enough has so that we are more than glad we came here and enormously grateful for our good fortune. We found that the twentieth century intrudes no matter where one lives, but there are good as well as disturbing aspects to that fact. We have learned that while there are some who envy us our life here, there are more who, although they think it wonderful to visit for a few months in summer, view the idea of year-round "isolation" with feelings ranging from apprehension to astonishment that we would deliberately elect it. As for us, whether the day dawns blue and brittle cold, or damp and foggy with a smoky southwester, we sing our morning hymn of gratitude.

The essays in this book, written and published week after week over a period of more than twelve years, are a picture of our lives and an expression of our philosophy, a philosophy that has matured and confirmed itself as the months and years have continued in their unhurried and inevitable course. We feel most fortunate to live in tranquility, but even more to associate daily with neighbors who are thoughtful and helpful, and who have no great interest in whether a man is rich or poor so long as he tends to his business and pulls his weight. It is refreshing to live where people have pride in themselves and their heritage, where the children wave to you unafraid, and the drivers of passing cars salute you on the theory that if they don't recognize you, they should.

To explain why, in this book, I use the terms "town" and "village" interchangeably, I should point out that the word "town" is merely a political definition in Maine and carries no suggestion of an urban area. We dwell, in a very true sense, in a village. Except for the church, school, post office, cemetery, firehouse, library, store, and Town office, all roughly localized near the harbor, our houses are scattered haphazardly along about fifteen miles of winding road.

Although lobstering, clamming, and scalloping are still important occupations, they are but a shadow of what they were 100 years ago. The price of lobsters is variable, but a lobster dinner now will cost you as much as a ton of lobsters did in the town's early days. The canneries and fish factories are gone, and the boatyards build nothing larger than pleasure craft and an occasional lobster boat. There are several house builders who, collectively, are the town's largest employers. Most of their work involves the building and maintenance of summer homes.

A measure of the numbers of our summer visitors is indicated by the

15

doubling of the town's population in July and August. Increasingly, people "from away" are taking up permanent residence, but not in sufficient numbers to affect the character of the town. The old names, descendants of the families who settled here in the eighteenth century, still dominate the town rolls and fill the phone book—and everyone hopes it will remain that way.

Our weather is what saves us from being overwhelmed. Those who contemplate coming here to live year-round hesitate when press and television report we are snow and icebound and isolated from civilization. Therein lies our safety. Actually we feel as the English did during one particularly horrendous storm when their newspapers headlined: CONTINENT ISOLATED. The weather never surprises us. If I awake in the night and hear the soft rasp of snow on the windows, I know that in a little while I shall see a blinking red light reflected on the ceiling and hear the rattle and grind of the snow plow, assuring me access to the outer world come the morning.

*To every thing
there is a season*

ECCLESIASTES

Life in the Country

I suppose any columnist, regardless of his field, hears from his readers promptly when he says something with which they violently disagree. In my case, because my subjects are usually noncontroversial rural matters of no earth-shaking importance, the letters I receive only rarely express indignation. Most of them come from people who say they enjoy what I write about country and garden matters, and they are reminded of the happy times of their youth. In spite of the urban explosion of the past fifty years, there are many people who were born on farms or at least in small country towns who are quick to express interest in Amen Farm and its animals and crops. I enjoy hearing from them and, though it takes time, get around to answering them all in due course. A good many tell me they like my periodic excursions into literature and rural philosophy, which pleases me because it tends to support my belief that there are many more thoughtful, literate people than a glance at television programming would suggest.

I am frequently asked how Amen Farm came by its name. The answer is that it was christened by my wife who, when we moved in, said "Amen. This is it!" And it will continue to be "it" because we are now past the age of wanting to move or to travel very far. It would be quite wrong, though, if the name gave the impression that Amen Farm is a farm in the sense that we gain our whole livelihood from it. We have other sources of income to prove the old adage that in order to make a living in Maine you need three or four jobs. I admit to having several, but even so I would not have anyone think that Amen Farm is just a name. Except for necessary staples, we feed ourselves almost entirely from its products. We have, at one time or another, operated a small dairy, using Guernseys and Brown Swiss milkers; raised several types of beef animals for meat, including Black Angus, Herefords, and Scotch Highland cattle; and raised, slaughtered, and clipped a few sheep. We have had a few pigs and have always kept chickens, the number varying from a dozen to a hundred. Not only because we enjoy fresh food, but because I have always been what the English call a "keen" gardener, we raise all of our own vegetables and most of our fruit. Needless to say, we also have a large flower garden.

A lot of visitors, both friends and strangers (I count all my readers as friends), stop by to see the source of my columns. Usually they express amazement that my wife and I take care of such a "big place" alone. I soon disabuse them of that notion because, like anyone who runs a farm, we employ help. The only way we could avoid doing so would be by being young and vigorous, which we are not, or by having a large family of sons and daughters to do the job, and ours are grown and flown long since.

Because we live in the deep country, we do not face the suburban hassle about finding people to work for us. Also, we do not view them in the way more sophisticated citizens do. Those few who help us are our neighbors and friends; were it necessary, and were we able, we would as lief work for them. One of the happiest rewards of living where we do is the knowledge that we are part of a community. We know that if we were in trouble and able to holler loud enough, we could stand in the middle of the road and yell and in no time half the town would show up to help out.

I suppose that could they figure how to do it, the I.R.S. would put half of us in jail for swapping goods or services with the other half, but they would be bucking a whole way of life. One of our neighbors is a topflight bread maker, so we swap eggs for bread. My wife said the other day that we were not giving her enough eggs for the amount of bread she was providing us. She replied that she was getting all the eggs she wanted, so what! I suggested that, as a way out, we could increase the price of our eggs until it balanced the price of bread, which amused us both. We also swap a few eggs for scallops in season.

People here are always giving each other something, without any particular end in view, because that is the way we live. We had a party not long ago at which we served mussels *marinière*. I was trying to figure out the tide so I could get some at low water, when a young friend showed up with a peck of them as a gift. I don't know yet what I am going to do for him, but sooner or later some opportunity will develop.

One of the principles of domestic country life is that if you are given something you never send the dish back empty. The custom grew up when nobody had much but, when they did have something, they shared whatever it was. Perhaps they had slaughtered an animal and could not use it all so they passed the excess around, and by and by their turn came to be on the receiving end. I have one neighbor who works in a fish cannery, packing sardines. Frequently, in season, mackerel get taken with the other fish. When that happens the packers get them, and I can be sure of a fresh mackerel for breakfast. For many years, another neighbor down the road a way unfailingly appeared in August with a large basket of blackberries. Not just a pint box, but several quarts. She has now grown too old to go blackberrying and lives in a city, but her generosity will remain as a pleasant memory as long as I live. On our side, we provide a good many high-bush blueberries in season, as well as other things in the horticultural or vegetable line.

From the farm and from my neighbors I get many invisible dividends, too, that I use in my column after working them over in my head as I lie awake at night looking at the stars. Anthony Trollope said anybody could write, that all you had to do was to take pen in hand (he lived before the days of typewriters) and write. He did. He wrote innumerable novels, some quite excellent that have been shown on television, but to me writing is a little more difficult than that. Writing, as he said, is simple enough—the trick is to find something to write about. I find my subjects, for the most part, around Amen Farm and, having them as a lead, sometimes discover myself on a magic carpet flying far out of sight of our pleasant green woods and pastures and vistas of blue water. I always come back, though, for here is home. Amen.

A Silent Trio

Most mornings, after I have eaten my breakfast and fed the animals, I walk down the hill under the birches and along by the alders to the rocky shore-line, accompanied by Quince and Butterscotch, our dog and cat. If the weather is bad, Butterscotch stays behind and watches out of the kitchen window. Fog or light drizzle does not deter him, but driving rain he will not venture into; and while he enjoys rolling in fluffy snow, he declines to walk in it. He takes a few steps, like a barefoot boy on a pebbly road, lifts his paws and shakes them after every step, and finally gives up and discon-solately watches his friends disappear down the hill.

I enjoy their companionship, and they seem to like mine. We are a silent trio. They do not bother me with speculations about things that cannot be changed, and I allow them to busy themselves about their lawful occasions.

Quince smells all the rocks and tufts of grass and trees that he has inspected a thousand times before, and he leaves his imprint upon them until he runs out of ink, after which he goes through the ceremony anyway. Butterscotch advances in a series of short bursts, galloping twenty feet or so and then rolling in the lane until we catch up with him. I do not think that a cat's nose is as keen as a dog's, but the cat is compensated by having a keener sense of hearing and, perhaps, also of sight. The slightest sound or movement in the bushes will put him on the alert.

I know that Butterscotch is a killer, for I find odd pieces of unconsumed birds and mice and chipmunks around the place. If he is adroit enough to knock down an unusually fine piece of game, he brings it home to show us before destroying the evidence. But that is his nature, just as it is mine to consume farm animals, so who am I to deny him?

Quince, on the other hand, never kills anything. He makes a great deal of noise and looks very menacing, but the wild things have nothing to fear from him. I have tried to shoot over him but he, not being properly trained, puts the birds up so far ahead that I would need to be carrying a rifle to reach them. He enjoys the sport, though, and points grouse or bumblebees with equal enthusiasm.

Quince was a grown dog when my wife shocked him by introducing a small ball of yellow fur into the household. It took him some time to get used to the idea, but Butterscotch, never having heard that dogs did not like cats, made affectionate gestures toward him and presently he was won over. I notice, however, that he still flinches when the cat walks under him, but that I excuse him. I am uneasy when small babies sit on my lap.

I am sorry for people who do not number animals among their friends. Not everyone can go to the barn, as I do, and have a cow reach out to lick his hand with obvious signs of greeting, but most who live in the country are able to have some domestic animal as a member of the household. The small cost of their keep, in food and attention, is repaid a thousandfold.

My only regret is that most of our animal friends have shorter lives than ours, and only the person who has lost the companionship of an old friend can comprehend the grief that accompanies their passing. Perhaps it is to remind us that we too are mortal, a fact that some seem to avoid, although death overtakes us all in the end.

*

Attic Rooms

Most boys brought up in the country, those my age anyway, have experienced sleeping in an attic bedroom. Attic bedrooms seem peculiarly appropriate for boys. Perhaps it is because boys are less likely, in such surroundings, to cause damage, or perhaps boys themselves elect to be away from the rest of the family so they can practice the mysteries of boyhood. So they can keep copies of *Huck Finn* and *Treasure Island* on a shelf by the bedside, where they can be seen, and hide treasures less literary under the eaves, where they will escape confiscation by female authority. I don't know what boys did in my day without *Playboy* and its imitators in the realm of sex literature (collected by my grandson from the age of about twelve), but they seem to have gone through life without their animal urges being stunted. The fact that there are grandsons around has to prove something.

Most attic bedrooms were equipped with skylights, which invariably leaked. Skylit bedrooms usually had a couple of pails, or perhaps a slopjar, in constant readiness to keep drips from soaking through the rough flooring and making spots on the ceiling of the room below.

The house I grew up in was quite ancient and had no neat plan of rooms drawn up by an architect. Bits and pieces had been added over the years, as new generations discovered new needs, so that several of the enclosures, in addition to serving as rooms, were also passages. The room I slept in was one such. To get at it I had to pass through something called the sewing room, although all it was ever used for was to store articles no one knew what to do with but could not bring themselves to throw away. The most useful thing in it was the "ragbag" that provided patches to cover holes in Junior's pants or odd scraps of material to contribute to someone engaged in that endless task of making a patchwork quilt.

The young, those in my social stratum anyway (and that seemed to me to be almost everybody), dressed in whatever old clothing happened to be around except, of course, on some special occasion. Overalls, frequently called "overhalls," were used by workmen, denim not yet having risen to its present dizzy social heights.

The idea of taking a kid to a shop and outfitting him for school every fall was unheard of. If the family was large, hand-me-downs served several children in turn; if not, one's own "good" suits were stretched out at the wrists and ankles until equatorial enlargement of the wearer made the job pointless. However, not many of us felt deprived. We were warm, clean, and patched; and we suffered, without too much pain, discipline that nowadays would be considered damaging to a child's psyche. What was devastating was to have to appear in anything new, but that did not happen very often. When it did, a little roughhousing from one's friends soon removed the curse.

To enter my quarters from the sewing room, anyone over six feet tall had to duck his head and keep it ducked, as that was the central height of the attic. A door at the other end opened into a closet which, in turn, let onto a landing from which the stairs descended to the kitchen. On the opposite side of the landing was another door to a small bedroom dignified with a gable-end window. My room had only a skylight. I thought it far preferable to an ordinary window.

Through it I could gaze at the heavenly bodies at night and the tops of the trees and the not infrequent rainclouds in the daylight hours, although to be truthful, I did not spend much of the day there unless I had been banished for infraction of the rules governing small boys' conduct. I was very fond of my room. By standing on my bed I could look down through the skylight onto the garden, and if work seemed in the offing I could remain quietly aloof. If, on the other hand, friends or food were in sight I could make a quick exit down the back stairs and through the kitchen, levying toll on anything edible within reach, and appear nonchalantly through the shrubbery as though I had just happened by.

In spite of their less-than-perfect reputation for being watertight, skylights have a charm not conferred by other fenestration. I have been reminded of this, after an adult lifetime of looking through conventional windows, because I have just had a skylight installed in my bedroom. It is, I must confess, a superior sort of skylight, having been imported from Denmark, where it is very popular. Denmark is a congested country, and I suppose about the only direction a Dane can look without seeing another Dane is straight up, hence the skylight's popularity. However, I did not have to go to Denmark—I bought mine in Portland.

The moment the new skylight was installed I was reminded of my boyhood. Until yesterday my room, though in every way comfortable and insulated against the winter blasts, had a feeling of confinement. When I awoke this morning I felt cradled in the clouds. The sun had not yet risen and the horizon was invisible in a carmine haze. Above it, Western Mountain floated, looking strangely small with its lower slopes hidden. I suppose I could have viewed the scene—same mountain, same clouds—through any ordinary window, but there is something about looking down on the world through a hole in the roof of one's house that separates one from workaday folk who spend their days confined behind vertical surfaces.

I know that many of my friends will think I have taken leave of my senses to be cutting holes in my roof just so I can see the world from a different angle but—I wonder? Doesn't everything that makes life exciting, intriguing, challenging, interesting, come from our being able, occasionally, to look at it all fresh and strange? The French have a phrase for it—*point d'appui,* a point of support, a fulcrum, with which, Archimedes remarked, one could move the world.

As I lay abed a crow scaled down from the sky, extended its flaps, air-braked in, and came to rest on the topmost point of a spruce tree I planted fifteen years ago. It is not everyone who has a chance to look down on a crow on the topmost twig of a spruce tree.

24

The Broken Thread

I don't know if the mild weather we have been experiencing during the past ten days can be dignified by the name of a January thaw, but I have a notion it is about all we are going to get.

Sunday was bright and the temperature rose enough for me to shovel out the snow that Saturday's storm had dumped into the driveway. Yesterday was dark and gloomy but not freezing, and water was still trickling off the roof and running in the little gutters in the cellar. Today continues dreary, with a cold rain pelting down since noon. I have been watching the thermometer and I have an idea the temperature will sink enough tonight to put a glaze of ice on the roads after the sun sets.

There is a lot to be said both for and against retirement, but to my mind one of its greatest delights is not being compelled to venture forth in bad weather. Of course one gets trapped occasionally and has to keep a dentist's appointment (which if cancelled won't be replaced for six months), but usually one can watch the snow accumulate from inside the window instead of from outside.

There are more retired people today than there have ever been, but somehow or another they seem to constitute a problem both to themselves and to society. There are books and magazine articles and television programs all purposefully endeavoring to solve the difficulties of the retired. Unhappily there is not much that can be done to win a race after the horse gets over the finish line. The time to prevent the problems of old age is before retirement, not after. If a person has had no interests outside his employment, particularly if he has had no intellectual interests, it is asking the impossible to suppose a well-rounded, self-sufficient character can be created after retirement.

The construction of modern society is against contentment and happiness for the retired, particularly if they live in one of the vast urban areas. In the country, even though it is not as it was a hundred years ago, the old and retired are still likely to be a part of the community. They do not find themselves suddenly discarded. They drift into old age, seeing their friends, participating in things they have always joined in, and continue a part of the small town or village where they have lived. When a man in a suburb is confronted with retirement he finds himself alone. The dormitory empties in the morning and he has nowhere to go nor anything significant to do. He takes the train into town a couple of times to lunch with his old pals, but soon finds he is unfamiliar with what they are discussing and realizes the thread that held them together is broken.

One of the worst things that can happen to a retiree is to live in one of the vast mausoleums that advertise themselves as communities for the elderly. It is good for neither young nor old to be segregated into age groups. I do not suggest that older people should accompany the young to rock festivals, but if they met together in the normal intercourse of family and village life, the generation gap we hear so much about would not be so wide.

I do not claim that if everyone took up gardening or some other hobby in early life the problem of what to do after retirement would be solved, but I do say that one cannot abruptly, on a given day, be bereft of one set of interests and immediately find another.

I believe a good deal of the blame for the situation can be laid at the feet of an educational system that has increasingly, over the last fifty years, devoted itself to teaching people how to make a living instead of teaching them how to live. This is the philosophy that the young are revolting against. I hope they are successful, because if they are not, they will one day be facing the same dreary prospect that presently confronts so many of their elders.

Three Below Zero with Wind

When I lifted the garage door this morning, a good part of three feet of snow that had drifted against it fell inside. Having shoveled that out, I contemplated, without enthusiasm, the 200 feet or so I was going to have to wade through to get to the barn. The temperature was three below zero, and the wind, blowing briskly, was swirling dry snow in eddies around every obstruction, scouring the ground bare in some places, and piling drifts in others.

I was not worried about the stock. As long as animals are well fed and watered they generate their own heat. All they need otherwise is a little shelter to protect them from the wind. They carry their insulation around with them. The three Scotch Highland cattle were standing, unconcernedly, in the lee of the barn with a blanket of ice and snow on their long shaggy coats. They had icicles hanging from their nostrils. When I opened the barn door, to throw out some hay, the bull got in my way. I tried to shove him off to one side with my pitchfork, but I might just as well have been pushing at the barn itself. A hayfork is not a very effective weapon with which to take on a bull that weighs more than half a ton and has hide an inch thick.

All he wanted was a little grain and he knew where it was kept. I could see I was not going to win the argument with a line buck, so I decided on an end run and threw a scoopful of grain out onto the snow. Almost before it landed he and the others were impolitely shoving each other around to get it. Water is a problem at three below. It freezes solid if there is not a heated trough, and there was not, so I gave it to them in a pail. They all drank in the proper pecking order: the bull first, the heifer second, and the little steer last.

The sheep, in the pasture, bleated mournfully. They were not hungry, they just wanted company. They were not interested in the pile of hay outside their shelter, nor were they about to get under cover. They were rummaging around under the snow and coming up once in a while with a few blades of dead grass that stuck out of their mouths, giving them a look of farmers chewing on straws. Sheep have peculiar eyes. They are fixed, and look as though they were made of smoked glass. I can see in my bull's eyes what he is thinking about, but a sheep's eyes are like opals with a line down the center. They never change expression.

On my way back to the house I made a courtesy call on the hens. Four of the five nest boxes were occupied, one of them by three birds. Two hens had sucked in their waistlines enough that by dint of much wriggling they had achieved a relatively horizontal position from which to drop their burden, while the third was perched like an uneasy gymnast on their backs. Why hens do this is an avian conundrum that I have, as yet, been unable to solve. Anyway, by coaxing and theft I managed to collect eighteen eggs. Rudy, who around here is not a red-nosed reindeer but a bantam rooster, made his usual pass at me on my way out. He is very circumspect, hiding among his harem until I turn my back, upon which he rushes at me with a bristling of his ruff and a sideways motion that stops as soon as I turn and face him. He is really nothing but a big phony. I let him get away with it for, as one male chauvinist relating to another, I don't want to embarrass him in front of his wives.

I don't hang around the barn long these days. When we had a few milch cows that lived in the tie-up during the winter it was pleasantly warm in there, but with the stock outside it is as cold as a vault. It reminds me of the story of Aunt Millie who died during a cold spell in the winter. They couldn't bury her, and the town didn't have a vault, so they stacked her in the woodshed. In the spring she came out as fresh as a haddock.

On the way back to the house I found the bird feeder crowned with a foot of snow that I swept off onto the ground. With it went quite a bit of seed that will be picked up by the ground feeders, particularly a dove that has been hanging around when he should be headed south. More sunflower seed was needed so I got some, but before I could empty it on the tray, a chickadee swept down onto my thumb to take his tribute. Chickadees and pine siskins seem to be the most trusting of wild birds. It takes very little patience to induce them to feed from your hand. I didn't linger, though. My patience evaporates pretty rapidly at three below.

Up March Hill

When the days climb one after another up "March Hill," as the time between Town Meeting and the first greening of the stream banks and spring holes is called hereabouts, a subtle change occurs in the landscape. It is quite invisible to those in a hurry but lifts the spirits of those who have eyes to see.

Nathaniel Hawthorne, one of the most sensitive of our writers, wrote, "Happiness is a butterfly which when pursued is always just beyond your grasp, but which, if you will sit down quietly may alight upon you." Early spring is like that. It is scarcely more tangible than the weight of a butterfly on your outstretched hand, and unless you pause quietly you will not know it is there at all.

The setting sun floods the room behind me with rosy light. As I look to the east, out of my small paned study window, the snowfields on the slopes of Western Mountain reflecting the sun are like pink handkerchiefs flung among the dark purple of the spruces. On the shoreline in front of me a grove of white birches is silhouetted against the still water of the bay. Within the last week, or so it seems, the lacy twiggery of their upper branches has turned from a winter brown to a soft faded barn red.

A willow I planted a few years ago in front of my cow yard is as yellow as butter. There are no buds yet, not even any swelling, but the color of the bark is startling against the snow. Down below the shore pasture is a large elderberry from which I am going to pilfer a few branches to force. The buds are already enormous, and just a few days in the kitchen will bring out the knobby purple flower heads. The poplars, "them damn popples," as a neighbor calls them, are swelling and can likewise be added to one's foretaste of spring. As the sun sinks behind the woodland, the maples are etched sharp against the sky, as they have been all winter, but I must enjoy the sight now, for soon they will be a haze of swollen buds.

Though the snow is still six feet deep where it was piled by the last storm, it is giving way in little brittle edges along the ground under the increasing strength of the sun. The long sweeping drifts across the hayfield are the shape of sand dunes, and change in color from pale pink to lavender as I watch them. Snow is seldom white, more often the color ladies call aqua, that is, water—and like water, reflects the color of its surroundings.

In the swamps, which remain unfrozen most of the winter, the skunk cabbages are piercing the muddy ground. As with many other plants, their growth is timed to the length of the day, and as the days lengthen, so do they, regardless of temperature.

My dog took me a walk this morning to where some pussy willows were growing in a roadside ditch. As I jumped across to pick some, a brace of grouse that had been feeding on wild apples exploded in my face.

A friend who came to Maine to live not long ago, told me his only regret was that he had not done so ten years earlier. He is a man of consequence and means, and could have had the best out of any city—but there are no pussy willows or partridges on Fifth Avenue.

The Shape of Life

This farm supports a lot more lives than those of its legal owners. I say legal owners, but it is only human vanity that says our rights are transcendent.

The others, the chipmunks and the squirrels, the foxes and the porcupines, the bobcats and the deer, the raccoons and the skunks, the mice and the rats, the hosts of birds of all species, and the myriad insects I know nothing of (as well as those that I do, like the mosquitoes and the black flies) all own the place by virtue of inheritance. Their ancestors have lived off the land ever since there has been any land.

We are Johnny-come-latelies and, though we have a deed that purports to give us sole right of ownership, we have no more rights than they have without any deed. What we have is a life tenancy, which is just what they have, and when we die we are just as dead as they are.

It is true that the majesty of the law, invented by man, permits us to be the sole judge of which humans take over our tenancy when we die or leave here, but our joint tenants care not what we do or if we do anything at all. They neither sweat nor worry nor strain. They take what comes and make the best of it, and if we could emulate them we should be able to lead happier and more contented lives.

Oh, I know that robins stake out their territory and hustle strangers off their worm patch, and I suppose other birds and animals do likewise, but they don't lay claim to the place in perpetuity as we do.

We humans have a strange hankering after immortality, a thing that every evidence of nature contradicts except to the extent that nothing is ever wasted and having run its cycle in one form eventually shows up again in another.

I have always been interested in graveyards; not big city cemeteries where the tombstones stand in serried ranks like suburban housing but small ones, such as that at Searsport, Maine, where the stones record that so-and-so died of yellow fever in the Sumatra Straits and was buried at sea.

They are a sign of man's struggle to repudiate the finality of death. Some graves are tended for quite a while, but time in the end conquers them all. The stones fall and are buried and forgotten, or are used to prop up a wall or pave a road. Some I know are engulfed by wild land, by spruces, alders, and puckerbrush.

I am interested in a little ancient graveyard, out here on the Point near where I live, and I have been collecting money to establish a fund to provide for "perpetual care." However, even as I do so, my sense of the ridiculous tends to overwhelm me. I say to myself, "Perpetual care. *Perpetual* care." My dictionary defines perpetual as "continuing or enduring forever," which, if you ponder upon it for a minute, is beyond the ken of human experience.

What we really are saying is that this world is such a wonderful place we can't bear to give it up and that, somehow or other, if we stake out a spot and put a marker on it, as my dog does here and there when he goes walking with me, we shall establish a perpetual right of re-entry. It's rather like leaving the shed door on the latch.

In the meantime our cotenants go on about their affairs enjoying every minute that they are here, fluting in the dawn, absorbing the warmth of the midday sun, and singing down the evening star, not worrying about things they know not of.

I do not believe I am being a Pollyanna when I suggest it is better to let the river of life find its own channel than to force it along in the way we think it should run. I believe that, given a chance, it is better to "roll with the punches" than to claim, as did William Henley in "Invictus," that:

> *In the fell clutch of circumstance,*
> *I have not winced nor cried aloud;*
> *Under the bludgeonings of chance*
> *My head is bloody, but unbowed.*

I believe too, as I believe nothing else, that man's greatest need today is for occasional solitude, time for contemplation, so that he can listen undistracted to that small inner voice that so rarely gets a chance to make itself heard.

Fog has hung over Naskeag Point every day now for more than two weeks. I could bemoan it and complain that it is mildewing my roses and spoiling my view. I have heard that an old woman who lives not far away sobbed—because, she said, the weather was so dreary, so dreadful, and so depressing. But I have noticed that the robins are finding a plentiful supply of worms, that the swallows are swooping low over the pasture gathering insects (blackflies, I hope), and that the wet leaves of my lilacs look varnished in the light from the kitchen windows.

Who am I to quarrel with the shape of life?

A Lift to the Spirit

When I was a young fellow at sea, those of us who held unlimited licenses (the ones issued by the Steamboat Inspection Service declaring that we were qualified to navigate vessels of any tonnage on any ocean) looked down our noses at men who held only a "coastwise" certificate. Dogs-bark navigators, we called them, asserting that the only reason they knew where they were in a fog was because they could distinguish the bark of one neighbor's dog from that of another. We were, however, glad to have one of them aboard when we got onto unfamiliar soundings in thick weather.

I have been reminded of them during the past month, when I could have used one to pilot me around my garden in the enveloping fog. When I went back to the vegetable garden yesterday, to get a couple of heads of lettuce, the tops of the spruce trees were out of sight in the clouds and a gull that was flying "contact" came past about a yard over my head, no more sure of his position than I. Although gulls will follow rivers and ponds inland, you have to live on the coast to have them as daily companions, which is one of the pleasures of being here.

Viewed at a distance, gulls are beautiful birds, particularly when in flight. They belong in the air, and it gives a lift to the spirit to see them coast downwind, then turn and breast the current and be borne aloft without moving a feather. They are, I think, the most universal of birds. Wherever you may be on the world's littoral you will find them, and if you come from Maine, they will call the heart home. At sea, far from land, they float along in the wake of deepwater vessels picking up any edible scraps that go overboard, and to a gull almost anything is edible. Along shore they cluster like a swarm of bees, crying and quarreling over the scallopers or lobstermen, while inland they will follow the plow as though it was a boat, examining the turning sod for worms or grubs.

I have never known gulls to damage a garden. They do steal scraps from the compost heap, but I do not begrudge them that small impost for the pleasure of their company. Most of all I like to see one sitting on my chimney. I am reminded of the pictures of storks nesting on the chimney pots in Germany, where they are thought to be omens of good fortune.

In the days of sail the old Navy used to put ship's cats on the Articles as mousers so that they could draw rations—though history does not divulge who drank their tot of rum. I think the Department of Tourism in Augusta should do the same for gulls; not only to reward them for the garbage they clean up, but for the attraction they are to our summer visitors. Wherever there are tourists to be found near salt water, there also will be found gulls. When I lived in Sullivan Harbor, one of our favorite drives was to Schoodic

Peninsula, particularly after an easterly storm, and there, in season, we could always find tourists feeding gulls.

I used to worry a bit about a gull snapping off someone's finger or hoisting a child aloft by the hand, as eagles were pictured as doing in the old woodcuts of my childhood, but nothing serious ever seems to happen. Perhaps after getting a good close look at a gull's beak, the sightseers become more cautious than they appear to be. For all its beauty in the air, a gull is a pretty tough customer and, like a goat, will eat almost anything it can swallow. Many times I have watched them gulp down the whole carapace of a lobster.

Gulls don't seem to worry about the weather. They take it as it comes, which is what we gardeners have to do also, whether we like it or not. My lilacs are mildewed, the petunias hang limp and brown, and the leaves of the young corn are as yellow as butter—but the snapdragons are flourishing, the delphiniums are six feet tall, and the peas are up to my knees. As the old circus men used to say, what you lose on the pretzels you make on the beer.

Saga of Belka

I had to perform a sad little duty yesterday. An old cat that has been a pensioner of this establishment for many years and has, of late, been living with my wife's mother, had come to her latter days. She had been suffering for some time from the same disabilities that most of us fall heir to in our old age: arthritis, misery of the stomach, and, recently, cataracts. She could no longer see and felt her way around by following along walls and furniture. In spite of her handicap she still tried to hunt, by ear, and Mom was first convinced of her blindness when she saw her pet jump at a bird and miss by a great distance and fall into the cold frame. It was this event that convinced us it would be a kindness to put her down, and was the reason I took her to the vet.

The cat was called Belka, a name given her by my Russian daughter-in-law. It is a Russian word meaning "squirrel" and was chosen because of her long, soft, gray hair. She was much like a squirrel in other ways, too, for she was always about half wild and never submitted willingly to caresses. The only person she would permit to touch her during the last few years of her life was my mother-in-law, who is also very old, so I suppose it was a community of age. Belka was eighteen which, I have been told, is the human equivalent of 126, an accumulation of years that not even Mom can compete with. I am a little dubious about the mathematical accuracy of equating seven years of a cat's life to one of a human's. It works out pretty well with small to middle-sized dogs (large dogs usually do not live so long), but I think that a multiplier of five or six years might be closer for cats. In any event, by any calculation, she was well stricken in years.

Belka's mother, a six-toed Maine shag, came to us when we lived in Sullivan about twenty-three years ago. We got her as a kitten from a household on Grindstone Neck, so she was born a summer person and continued so, for we were then living part-time in Pennsylvania and only brought her back to Maine in summer. We named her Boxy because she had feet like boxing gloves. How she could have mothered as fey a cat as Belka is hard to understand, because she was most lovable and got along with everyone, even the then-current warden of the house, a Scottie named Lanky. He was a bit dubious when we introduced them, but she soon had him won over and when she produced her first litter, employed him as a baby-sitter.

It has been my experience that cats and dogs, with the proper introduction, soon learn to get along very well together and, in fact, some cats will take on canine habits, although I have not noticed that the reverse is true. Boxy and Lanky would go hunting together and would accompany me on walks, although Boxy preferred to walk along the tops of walls and fences while Lanky liked to keep all four feet on the ground. She would answer, though, to a whistle, just as he would, but her interest span was less, which I think is true generally of cats. All the dogs I have ever had the privilege of having live with me would accompany me for hours if I chose to stay out so long, whereas cats get tired after a while and either decide they have had it and turn around and go home or, as is the case with our present pussy, ask to be carried.

When Boxy was about to go into her first accouchement, she wandered around, as cats do, looking for a suitable spot to get on with the business. My wife was interested in this operation because she wanted to see the kittens born. She said she had never seen anything born and, when I asked her where she was when her own children appeared, replied that she was too busy, and that anyway delivery rooms were not equipped with mirrors. In true feline fashion, Boxy refused all offerings of cushions and blankets and in due course decided upon the hole in Helen's desk where the typewriter lives when it is not in use.

That night, when I got home, there was Boxy with half a dozen small wet objects with closed eyes and no apparent ears. When I made cheerful inquiry about the day's activities Helen said she had not seen a thing. She had worked at her typewriter all day, periodically looking under the desk. Whenever she looked there was another kitten, but Boxy, in her modesty, concealed the exact moment of arrival. Among this litter was a scrawny little runt that became known as Belka.

I know little about the paternal side of Belka's ancestry. Her mother was, like the earthworms described by eighteenth-century author Gilbert White, much addicted to venery, and accepted advances from total strangers. From the sounds that floated on the midnight air she either enjoyed herself immensely or was having a horrible time, but being unskilled in feline philology I was unable to determine which. In any event she always presented us with a healthy but varied lot of children.

Belka's early years were traumatic. My daughter-in-law fell in love with her and took her home to live with two very little girls who also fell in love with her. They expressed their affection by clutching her in a deathlike grip in an effort to thrust her into a doll carriage. Being wise, as cats are, Belka soon learned not to struggle but, as soon as her tormentors' backs were turned, leapt out and fled under the nearest piece of furniture. The little girls would go screaming after her and winkle her out of her fastness to go through the same procedure for the 100th or 500th time. Little wonder then that, subsequently, when they had all spent a vacation in Maine and were about to go home Belka vanished under a cottage and refused to reappear. There were no sticks long enough to sweep her out and no cajoling could induce her to appear voluntarily. Time, in its usual fashion, ran out and they had to leave. The last words to be spoken were those of my daughter-in-law as she crouched peering under the house. "Okay, stay there; I hope you die—*dead.*"

Belka did not "die dead," but lived for another sixteen years and, in fact, I had to "dead" her (as one of my small acquaintances accused me of doing to a hen we had for dinner); but Belka never recovered from her fear of children and fled incontinently whenever she heard a childish voice. She never again left Maine, either.

I was not overwhelmed by sorrow as I am when a dog who has been part of my household for many years comes to the end of his days. Although I am fond of all domestic animals, and treat them kindly (for they are all a part of God's creation just as am I), nevertheless I can view a cat's passing more dispassionately. It was also difficult to feel deep sorrow about the departure of an animal that had never responded to my overtures of friendship, even though I knew the cause of its trauma.

C. S. Lewis, who is best known in this country as the author of *The Screwtape Letters,* made a point. In a letter he once wrote, he said:

We were talking about cats and dogs the other day and decided that both have consciences but the dog, being an honest humble person, always has a bad one, but the cat is a Pharisee and always

*has a good one. When he sits and stares you out of countenance
he is thanking God that he is not as one of these dogs, or these
humans, or even as these other cats!*

I guess that covers it.

Less Given to Mass Homicide

When I went to the barn this morning to feed the heifer calf, I found she had upset her water during the night. As soon as I filled the pail she did it again, and when I tried once more she pretended she was going to charge me—but as I didn't move she capered off around the little barnyard with her tail held erect, as stiff as a flagpole, bucking like an unbroken colt. When she had had her fun she came to me sedately and drank and allowed me to scratch behind her ears.

I didn't feel like cutting any green feed, so I climbed into the mow and pitched down a bale of hay to shake out for her. The barn swallows were up there in force. Usually we take the window out of the gable so they still have access when the barn doors are closed. When I asked Albert if he had tended to it this year, he said he had not because there was a window broken and the swallows were using it for their excursions. I could not see it from where I stood in the dusty light, so I climbed up on the baled hay and sure enough it was broken, but the opening was not more than three inches wide at the bottom and tapered off to nothing below the muntin. The birds were complaining noisily about my presence, but I knew if I sat still for a few minutes they would ignore me and go off about their lawful occasions, and they soon did. The hole looked very small and there was no platform to alight upon, but swallows are marvelously adroit. They came at it under full power, and a fraction of a second before arriving, folded their wings and shot through like bullets.

What interested me most was that they were not building nests or feeding young but just seemed to be flying in and out for fun. Just having a good time. A half-dozen birds would be sitting shoulder to shoulder on a rafter, chattering away like a women's bridge club, when suddenly they would all take off, swoop around overhead a couple of times to gain momentum, and then flash, one after another, through the break in the pane of glass. In no time all or most of them would come hurtling back through the hole and bunch up on the rafter to play the next hand.

36

Whenever I watch swallows I am reminded of Gilbert White, to whom they were a constant fascination. In his day there was not only more leisure for country gentlemen to devote their time to such matters, but also (what we lack) an absorbing interest in what went on around them. Gilbert White was, of course, exceptional, but he had several correspondents who were equally interested in natural history, and from his writing it is easy to see that the ordinary, hardworking, eighteenth-century country laborer was also observant.

I never tire of watching animals at play. They are so like children in their antics that the fact that we are all members of the same creation is inescapable. A few years ago, when I had sheep in the shore pasture, I had occasion to go out one moonlit night. Our pasture, like most in coastal Maine, is liberally studded with boulders, and the lambs were playing "I'm the king of the castle," jumping from one rock to another, trying to dislodge the "king" momentarily on the high spot. I have seen children playing the same game many times. When the lambs found I was watching, they scrambled down and began to graze, as though they were ashamed of being caught playing when they should have been in bed asleep.

I suppose if you live in a city you must be guided by Alexander Pope's injunction that "The proper study of mankind is man," but if you are lucky enough to spend your days in the country, you can observe the animals, who are equally interesting and much less given to mass homicide.

Ginger Jars and Potpourri

On an old Pennsylvania blanket chest that stands against the wall in my library are two large Chinese ginger jars. I do not know whether the decorations on them are supposed to represent flowers or butterflies, as the artist who painted them, many years ago, worked with a flowing hand and was more concerned with beauty than with botanical or lepidopteran accuracy.

Most people who see them want to find out what is inside. Either openly or furtively they lift a lid and are at once enveloped in a haunting fragrance, for the jars no longer contain ginger but potpourri. I have owned them for a score of years and, so far as I can recollect, there has been no lessening of the aroma.

In years past, making potpourri was a favorite occupation of the ladies of the house. It was not difficult, taking only a little time and patience and a few easily obtainable ingredients. It is sad that this pleasant task has been allowed to become one of the vanished arts of a more gentle and less hurried day.

In addition to potpourri that was usually kept in a jar (as is mine), lavender and rosemary and scented geraniums, verbena, bergamot, lads-love, and other sweet-smelling leaves and flowers were collected and dried and sewed into little sachets, usually of satin, that were placed in drawers where linens and lingerie were kept. Alice Morse Earle, who probably knew more about home and garden life in the eighteenth and early nineteenth centuries than any other writer, used to stuff silken saddlebags with fragrant leaves to hang on the backs of her chairs or to slip between the cushions.

There are many recipes for making potpourri, for it is like cooking in that if you don't have one thing you substitute another. As everyone knows, all a good cook needs is a quick look at a recipe and she can take off from there, adventuring and changing, tasting and smelling, and soon winding up with her own version that is often better than the original.

In my garden library I have at least a dozen potpourri recipes, all a little bit different. Nevertheless, there are certain basic ingredients common to all, like oil and vinegar in a salad dressing. These are rose petals and salt, and as you need a lot of rose petals you should begin to collect them early in the summer.

One can make either a dry or a wet potpourri. It is called wet, but damp would be a better description. The dry type is more modern and more difficult to make, but it is prettier, as the petals retain their color. However, if you are going to put it in a jar like mine this distinction doesn't matter, because you can't see the potpourri anyway.

Here is a recipe of Alice Morse Earle's:

Take equal parts of fine table salt and powdered borax and one-tenth part of ground cinnamon. Mix well, and to every quart of rose petals add one dessert spoonful of the mixture. Mix well once or twice a day, adding dry scented geranium leaves, lemon verbena, lavender, thyme, rosemary, mint, and other sweet-smelling herbs, and adding more of the mixture in proportion.

Another recipe is:

Gather early in the day when perfectly dry a peck of roses, pick off the petals and cover them with three-quarters pound of common salt. Leave them for seven days and if fresh flowers are added, add also the right proportion of salt. Mix together one-half pound finely powdered bay salt, and the same quantity of spice, cloves, brown

sugar; four ounces gum benzoin and two ounces of powdered
orrisroot. [An old-fashioned druggist can get the orrisroot and
benzoin for you.] Add a gill of brandy and any sort of fragrant
leaves or flowers such as orange, lemon, lavender, verbena, thyme,
mint, or rosemary. They must be perfectly dry. The mixture must be
kept well stirred. If it gets too dry add more brandy.

As you can see, the recipes are pretty freewheeling. You can adjust them to suit what you have on hand. If you don't like brandy in your potpourri, you may add a little more salt. If the mixture seems too wet, more orrisroot will dry it. Orrisroot is the powdered root of an iris, *I. florentina* to be exact. It smells of violets and also helps fix the other fragrances.

One of my books says that you should crush old pomanders and add them to the potpourri. To make a pomander, cloves should be inserted into an orange so close together that the heads hide the skin of the orange. Four or five pomanders will scent a whole room. The orange will never decay and the pomander will get harder and harder the longer you keep it, until finally you can crush it and add it to your potpourri.

Long years ago ladies (and gentlemen too) used to carry pomanders in pierced containers to sniff when the smell of the canaille got too hard to take. There have been times in my own life when I would have been glad to have one.

Cellar Holes and Cinnamon Roses

A narrow, winding dirt road, almost closed in overhead by encroaching trees, with alders pushing out into the roadside ditches, branches, nearly undetected, off the highway near my farm. An observant person would notice that once, in days long past, the land bordering this road was cultivated. Stone walls, or fences as they are usually called in New England, thrown down by the frosts of many winters, are to be seen lying green and lichen-covered in the shade of the woodland that has reclaimed the old scanty fields.

The land was never good for anything but pasture, pretty snug pasture at that. The cows and sheep, getting a bite here and there as they were able, wandered among the boulders that were too large to be budged by the ox teams that cleared the land. There were never very many people living here, and now one can walk for miles and not see a house, though there is an occasional semblance of a clearing. There may also be a few gnarled and broken apple trees appearing to have been planted in rows instead of growing all a-kilter as wild ones do.

If you climb over the high roadside bank into one of these sad remnants of man's labor, you are likely to find a cellar hole, or at least some stones laid as a rough foundation. There will be a lilac and, if the dooryard has any open sky above it to let sunlight in, perhaps a cinnamon rose. I know one such spot where the rose has established a claim to the entire cleared space between the cellar hole and the road. The land is so poor, just sand and ledge, that the rose looks more like a ground cover than a shrub, but it still remains unconquered after who knows how many years.

Aside from its antiquity and its fierce will to live, the cinnamon rose has not much to recommend it, but those qualities were admired by people who settled this stern and bitter land. They had little time to devote to cosseting weaklings, either human or horticultural, so they gave it a place in their gardens. The flowers of *rosa cinnamomea* occasionally are single but more often double, and of a magenta pink. They come very early on a small-leaved, very prickly plant, which all my reference books say grows five to seven feet tall. Personally I have never come across any over a few feet, three at the outside, and usually lower.

Rosa cinnamomea is an old friend. It shared my garden when I lived in a little old house at Sullivan Harbor. The building was perched upon a rocky hillside overlooking Frenchman's Bay, and I was never sure whether the house kept the roses from sliding down onto the highway or whether the binding and tenacious roots of the roses saved the building from the same fate. The leaves, or the flowers—some say one and some say the other—are supposed to give off an odor of cinnamon. I have never been able to detect it, but fragrance or not, it is a curious old rose that has inhabited local gardens since Colonial days and is mentioned often in Sarah Orne Jewett's colorful stories of Maine. Two other shrubs that she unfailingly refers to are the snowberry and the syringa. These are both long-lived plants still to be found in many an old garden.

The snowberry is usually seen as a sparse and untidy low shrub covered with white berries. Because it will endure neglect and survive in the shade, that is usually its fate and where it is to be found. Given a little kinder cultivation, both the plant and its berries are much larger and well repay the little extra attention. The flower arranging ladies love it.

The shrub that Sarah Jewett refers to as a syringa is better known today as a mock orange. Actually the name *Syringa* is the botanical name of the lilac, and is a good example of the confusion that arises by the use of common names. The mock orange, or as Miss J. identifies it, the syringa, is properly a *Philadelphus*. Both are antiques and confer upon ancient door-yards the same feelings of times long past that boxwood does to gardens in more favored climes, and they are welcome for that reason.

Dawn

When I awoke and stood by my bedroom window this morning, dawn was just beginning to reveal distant objects. The back hayfield was silvered over with night mist that undulated along the contour of the land about three feet above it. Halfway between the back of the garden and the woods were two deer seemingly swimming, as their legs were invisible. When they bent over to graze, their heads disappeared also, so that their bodies might then have been mistaken for large boulders. Half an hour later they were gone, for except in early spring, deer do not wander about in the open after the light strengthens.

It is sad that city dwellers are not able to experience the freshness of dawn. During those years when I was compelled by business to travel, I always hated hotels that served breakfast in rooms still stinking from the previous night's tobacco. Whole cities smell so in comparison with the clean air of a country morning.

I am no longer outdoors much before seven o'clock, but I come down-stairs earlier, in my bathrobe, and open the door at first light so I can catch the magic of the moment and listen to the bird chorus. The earliest reveille hereabout is sounded not by the rooster but by the robin, with a plaintive woodland obbligato from the white-throated sparrow.

Some flowers need the heat of the sun to distill their fragrance, but flowering tobacco is never so sweet as in the half-light of dawn. The great fragrant, shadowy cups of moonvine, open all night, close at the first touch of the sun. Most night-blooming plants are pale in color, and fragrant, to attract moths and other night-flying insects to pollinate them. One of the most highly scented is the night-blooming stock. It has only drab lavender flowers, but they open to emit a most haunting fragrance. Other night-bloomers include the old-fashioned marvel-of-Peru, of our grandmothers' gardens, the evening primrose, and many of the honeysuckles.

When I stepped out early this morning I was accompanied by our new puppy, Happy, a little eight-week-old Brittany spaniel. She came to us from

South Carolina, and when I met her at the airport a few days ago I found her in her "sky kennel," patiently waiting for someone to claim her. I wish everyone I know could be so filled with wonder and delight as is she at each unfolding day. On the way home she slept on my lap, for she was tired and frightened, but that is all behind her now and every minute is pure joy. This morning she saw, for the first time, the fairy handkerchiefs that spiders scatter across the lawn each night to catch the morning dew. She sniffed the first one and started back in surprise as it vanished in front of her. Soon she found another, and then another, and each time the same thing happened. Almost at once it became a game, and she rushed around on the grass seeking new toys to play with.

Henry Thoreau once wrote that we should never forget that "we have lived not in proportion to the number of years that we have spent on the earth, but in proportion as we have enjoyed them."

He also said, "An early morning walk is a blessing for the whole day," and so is standing quietly to watch a new day flood silently over the world. Would that more of us had the time to so do, and that more who have the time would embrace the opportunity.

"Stag at Bay"

When I was a child I had the good fortune to have access to two good libraries. One was in the village, the benefaction of some Victorian landowner, and was under the jurisdiction of the parish church; the other was owned by my grandfather with whom I lived. I had free access to both, and I cannot remember being forbidden any book I wanted to read. True, Grandfather had a locked bookcase, but the lock was not designed to keep out an inquiring mind; it was there merely because there were some valuable books on the shelves. I recall that he had what I learned later was a first edition of Bunyan's *Pilgrim's Progress;* it would, I imagine, be worth a lot of money today. It was a bit heavy for me at the time, but I read it subsequently with enjoyment.

Grandfather was an outdoor man and owned several farms that, in the manner of the day, were let on long leases. He was a short, abrupt, no-nonsense man and spent a good part of every day in the saddle, keeping an eye on his property. Except in the evening, he lived in riding breeches and leather leggings, and always trailed an aroma of brandy and cigars behind him like the contrail of an airplane. He seemed an unlikely man to be possessed of literary interests, but he had several facets to his life, and one of them was a love of books, which was why he indulged himself with a library. I do not know how large it was (it seemed enormous to me), but I suppose, at a guess, it was 2,000 or 3,000 volumes.

Every library, other than a public one, reflects the taste of the owner, colored by the times in which he lives. Grandfather had the uniformly bound sets typical of his period, the sort of thing interior decorators now install along with the draperies, but while he must have been conscious that they looked well, *his* books were there to be read. It was in his study that I hurried my way breathlessly through the Waverley Novels of Sir Walter Scott, all umpteen volumes of them; Anthony Trollope's Barchester series (I couldn't handle the political novels); and of course Dickens, Thackeray, Kipling, and Rider Haggard, as well as the schoolboy stories of Ballantyne and Henty, which I know now were bought for my benefit. I was, and am, an omnivorous reader. My wife says if there is nothing else available I read the stories on the packets of sugar in restaurants.

Grandfather's library, reflecting his life, leaned heavily toward books about the country. He loved to ride and fish and shoot, and his shelves reflected those interests just as mine reflect my love of gardens. He must have had everything that had ever been put on paper about sport, from *The Compleat Angler* and *Hawker on Shooting* to the most current publications on how to raise pheasants and partridges, and how to tie flies. Sport for him did not mean commercialized sport; he would not have understood people being paid to play games and would, I know, have viewed it with contempt. Anyway, such a thing, happily, did not exist in his day.

He owned all of Richard Jefferies' country books (they were published in the 1890s when he was an old man), and he had them bound as they were available. He was familiar with Borrow, and Cobbett, and Gilbert White, and everyone else who had ever written about the outdoors.

Although he was not a talkative man, and would have scorned the modern notion that a man should be a "pal" to his children, he taught me a very great deal by example. When I was ten or twelve I went riding with him and he taught me to fish and shoot. I can still remember one terrible day when he caught me climbing over a fence without first "breaking" my gun. He unloaded it, relieved me of my ammunition and sent me home immediately in disgrace. I have never committed *that* sin again. His guiding star was politeness, and he did his best to instill in me the belief that being impolite (which included any lack of consideration for others) was inexcusable, and that a gentleman never raised his voice or lost his temper no matter what the provocation.

43

Even though my enthusiasms differ a little from his, I can look over my own library shelves and close my eyes and be back in those placid days before World War I (when we all thought the world was, except for a few unfortunate lapses, growing more civilized) and see once again the dark walls of his study, the chimney piece with Landseer's "Stag at Bay" hanging over it, and the rug where I lay on my stomach reading endlessly, and I can smell again the aroma of tobacco and brandy.

Neither of my grandfather's indulgences shortened his life. Born in 1835, he lived into the time of World War I and died, as his ancestors for several generations before him had done, in the house in which he was born. If anything could be said to have killed him, it was the war, which took from him many of the things he had believed immutable.

The war also took me, and I know now what a great sorrow that must have been to him. He said nothing about it, though, and when I went off to serve he took me to his club in London and gave me dinner, accompanied by a bottle of Meursault (which is still my favorite wine), and afterwards I had a whiskey and he his invariable brandy. We said good-bye just as though I was going off to school. His last words were, "We'll get some shooting this autumn . . . ." We did, but mine was different from his and he was not by my side. I was absent for a long time, longer than either of us had expected, and when I did return he was gone forever.

Hail to September

When I tore a page from the calendar that, by courtesy of Tamworth Farms Dairy, graces the wall of my study, I found it was September and that, praise be to God, tomorrow will be Labor Day. To many this may not seem an occasion for rejoicing, but to me it will signal less congestion on the highways, fewer people in the supermarkets, and a gradual diminution of visitors who, while I love them, cause me to eat too much and work too little.

The picture on the calendar is of a lobster boat, high and dry, alongside a short pier that supports a bait house and a gaggle of lobster traps. Behind the house are a few trees, oaks by their appearance, turning bronze and supplying a pleasant backdrop. Apart from the fact that self-respecting lobstermen don't let their boats shoal out at low water unless they are doing some work on the bottom (which in this instance was not the case) and the additional problem that oak trees do not color in September, it is an at-

44

tractive picture. Anyhow, it reminded me that autumn, although it does not officially arrive until September twenty-first, is not far around the corner— a fact that is confirmed by the color of the berries on the five rowan trees growing beside the stone wall separating my domain from the highway.

As an octogenerian I suppose I should be reminded of my approaching dissolution by the running down of the year and be feeling sad and threatened; but though it would make a good subject for an essay to be sold for the benefit of some pressure group of "senior citizens," I don't intend to write it because I don't feel sad at all. Anyway, to hell with the senior citizens, apart from those who are ill, disabled, or broke, because being old is all in one's head. In passing, it is worthwhile remembering that the young and the middle-aged can be ill, disabled, and broke, too.

I enjoy autumn. It is a time when the harvest is ready to be gathered in, if there is any harvest, which depends on how well you cultivated your garden—the one in your head as well as the one in your backyard. Cornelius Weygandt wrote a book toward the end of his life entitled *On the Edge of Evening,* which is a testament to the harvest of the mind. He was a professor in the English Department at the University of Pennsylvania and the most notable they have had. He wrote eighteen books, most of them about Pennsylvania or New Hampshire. I own sixteen, which some might feel suggests a small degree of partiality on my part, an accusation I would not dispute.

Years ago I attended the Wharton School, briefly, to brush up on some insurance subjects. I heard about "Corny," found out where he was lecturing and, when I could, stole into the back of the room as an observer. I am sure he soon discovered I was an intruder, but he never directed a question to me and never spoke to me until the end of the course. There was a certain milling about as the class broke up that gave him the opportunity to overtake me, and as he did he turned to me with a smile and asked, "Well, did you enjoy it?"

Although I have never been a full-time professional writer in the sense that I would have starved if I had not been paid for my writing, I have written a good deal. In what I have written I have always tried to remember Professor Weygandt's injunction that "No man is really writing until something within him of which he is no more than half conscious takes charge of him and inspires what he writes." I have learned also, out of my own experience, that the way to find that "something" is to plant one's backside firmly upon a chair in front of one's typewriter and begin to write. Corny's final testament is one in which, having in his earlier books harvested the heavy richness of the garden, he wanders around picking up the scattered sweet remainders of the year.

September is the beginning of the end, although it will be six weeks yet before a heavy frost blackens the hardier plants. The phlox and the dahlias are still going strong, but the fall asters and the goldenrod are showing color, and here and there an injured maple is pretending it is October. The sweet peas and the dahlias in the cutting garden are so plentiful that I cannot keep them picked; the tops of the onions begin to fall; the brussels sprouts are swelling; the beets and turnips and carrots are pushing their shoulders out of the ground; the peppers and eggplant (which the French call *aubergines,* a lovely word) are borne down by the weight of their fruit; the rows of lettuce, five varieties, are handsome enough to be used as centerpieces on dining tables; and the half-dozen russet apples I have been guarding all summer begin to look like those I remember as an apple-stealing schoolboy.

Two essays I read with affection every fall are "Autumnal Tints" and "Wild Apples," which were originally given as lectures by Henry David Thoreau and subsequently printed in *The Atlantic Monthly.* The former appeared in the October issue and the latter in the November issue in 1862. He had died on May sixth of that year.

In the Thoreauvian renaissance that has surfaced during the last quarter of a century, too much has been made of his social philosophy, or what his enthusiasts have thought was his social philosophy, and not enough has been recollected of his love of nature. To listen to his modern disciples one would conclude that he walked through the woods thinking of nothing but social causes, even though the great bulk of his writings are given over to other matters. Everyone has stolen from him what best suited their purpose and ignored the rest. F.D.R.'s famous "The only thing we have to fear is fear itself" was a variation on Thoreau with no credit line attached.

The two essays I have mentioned should be read by everyone who loves the country, particularly those who are enjoying two autumns, their own and nature's. The essay on autumnal tints ends with, "We cannot see anything until we are possessed with the idea of it, take it into our heads, and then we can hardly see anything else." In "Wild Apples" he quickly contradicts those who would have one believe that he is nothing but a humorless critic of society. Listen as he names the wild apples:

Let us enumerate a few of these. I find myself compelled, after all, to give the Latin names of some for the benefit of those who live where English is not spoken . . . There is . . . the apple that grows in an old Cellar Hole (Malus cellaris) . . . the Truant's Apple (cessatoris) which no boy will ever go by without knocking off some . . . The Frozen Thawed (gelato soluta) good only in that state . . . The Green Apple (Malus viridis)—this has many synonymes; in an imperfect state, it is the Cholera morbifera aut dysenterifera, puerulis dilectissima.

Now the rain begins to fall. Blessed rain that we have yearned for, for weeks. The autumn rain that will make green the grass, revive the flowers, and fill the wells. Hail to September.

The Fruitful Season

I have never been able to decide whether September is summer or autumn. In the middle of the day it *is* summer, but evenings and nights grow cold. By the end of the month the temperature of the ground is falling as a result of the longer nights. Soon, the residual heat of the summer is insufficient to compensate for the shorter days, and frost shows in the hollows when we go abroad in the morning.

I prefer to think of September as autumn, for to me it is the loveliest time of the year. I know there are some who shrink from the fall as a forerunner of winter, but I have taught myself not to look too far ahead. I enjoy what is at hand, like the katydids that chirrup merrily until that day when the sun has not enough warmth to quicken their cold limbs.

Thoreau said of September:

The increasing scarlet and yellow tints around the meadows and river remind me of the opening of a vast flower bud; they are the petals of its corolla, which are of the width of the valleys. It is the flower of autumn whose expanding bud just begins to blush. As yet, however, in the forest there are very few changes of foliage.

Most of the color of September is in the fields where the goldenrod and the fall asters (I like the English name for them, Michaelmas daisies; that is to say, the daisies of Michael's Mass, which is celebrated on September 29), the black-eyed susans, the blue of the chicory, the boneset, and all the shades of color in the ripening grasses begin to blend into an autumn palette.

We think of fall color being paced by latitude, and to an extent it is, but altitude also has a lot to do with it, as does the specific tree or plant providing the color. On my way to Pennsylvania one autumn day, I found the dogwoods already turning color along the Connecticut parkways. I suppose if they grew in Maine they would show change even sooner.

Then there is the ripening of fruit that September heralds: peaches, pears, and apples; pumpkins and winter squash, blue-gray and gold, in piles along the highway; and the scarlet of tomatoes piled on stands hung with bunches of orange bittersweet. It is as though all the lushness of summer had come to fruition at once.

Not long ago I planted a white peach tree in the garden of my little log house in southern Pennsylvania. Recently, when my wife went into the kitchen and opened the refrigerator, she found a dish of peaches awaiting us. Our daughter had picked them on Labor Day just as they began to fall, dead ripe, from the tree. Their fragrance spilled like nectar into the room.

I don't know why it is so difficult to buy white peaches nowadays. When I was young they were considered far superior to the yellow peach, and few people would buy a yellow peach if they could get a white one. I still think the white peach is a better fruit. The flavor is more delicate, somewhat reminiscent of almonds, and the flesh is more tender. The fruit is not as obese as a Hale or an Elberta. It is more aristocratic in every way with its pale greenish-white skin suffused with pink and rose on the sunny side.

I suppose white peaches do not ship as well as the yellow ones, for I have never seen a white peach on a stand outside of the South. Or perhaps Northerners no longer eat white peaches, just as the inhabitants of some cities refuse white eggs. Perhaps that goes for corn, too. When I was a boy, no one would eat yellow corn—it was considered to be fit only for horses. The favorite varieties were white: Stowells Evergreen, or Shoepeg, which was also known as Country Gentleman. They tasted about the same, but Shoepeg had the kernels placed irregularly on the cob. I will admit that they both had to be picked at exactly the right time to be tender, but they did not all ripen at once as do the modern hybrids. Instead, you could pick from a stand of corn for several weeks. The first acceptable yellow corn was Golden Bantam.

So much of the produce offered today, with fewer and fewer people living in the country and more and more in the cities, is determined by whether it ships well. During much of the year, city markets are dependent upon produce grown thousands of miles away, picked weeks before the consumer sets eyes upon it, and gathered long before it is ripe. I have bought peaches and melons and tomatoes that were stone hard and completely lacking in flavor. Fruit picked so green never does ripen. If you keep it long enough, it finally gets soft as a preliminary stage to decay.

Those of us who live in the country and have our own gardens and a few fruit trees, or are able to buy from a farm stand, can still taste fruit and vegetables as they should be eaten. September is the time to harvest one's own or to go out into the countryside to the source of supply. Fall in eastern America lingers on and on, long after the frost is on the pumpkin, so I vote to consider September as an autumn month, to make that fruitful season as long as possible.

"Life is Sweet, Brother"

I have only a little trouble with the Tenth Commandment. I am perfectly satisfied with my own house, as I am with my own wife, so I do not covet those of my neighbor. Insofar as menservants and maidservants are concerned, they are a vanishing species, and in Maine if you were to so call them you would not have any. Around here it is your neighbors who come in to give you a hand when you are too old or sick or busy to do things yourself. Oxen and asses have we none. The last draft oxen I was on speaking terms with were owned by the Howe brothers, Walter and Oscar, who farmed on Howe Hill outside Camden, Maine, and that was about thirty-five years ago. There is, of course, the final catchall phrase, which sounds as though it had been added by a lawyer, "nor anything that is thy neighbor's," that I stumble over.

My covetousness runs to things like a view; plants in other people's gardens (some of them); and the vigor I once possessed that is now the property of my juniors, who use it, as I did at their age, in pursuit of members of the opposite sex. About the only thing I really covet is more time to enjoy the common things that are the possession of everyone, the blessings that Jasper Petulengro recited:

> *"Life is sweet, brother."*
> *"Do you think so?"*
> *"Think so! There's night and day, brother, both sweet things; sun, moon and stars, brother, all sweet things; there's likewise a wind on the heath. Life is very sweet, brother; who would wish to die?"*
> *"I would wish to die—"*
> *"You talk like a Gorgio—which is the same as talking like a fool. Were you a Romany Chal, you would talk wiser. Wish to die, indeed! A Romany Chal would wish to live for ever!"*
> *"In sickness, Jasper?"*
> *"There's the sun and stars, brother."*
> *"In blindness, Jasper?"*
> *"There's the wind on the heath, brother...."*

The best things in life are free to everyone. Not even the "nor anything that is thy neighbor's" can trip you, for no one has freehold title to the sunset. Or perhaps we all have a joint tenancy, so that it is as much ours as it is our neighbor's.

One day in the midst of summer I was climbing Howe Hill. It is steep enough if you come up from the lower road through the juniper-studded pasture, and not much easier (and much longer) if you follow the road. I stopped here and there as I climbed to gather juniper berries (they are wonderful to season butter to baste squab or Cornish hen) and, looking up, perceived two oxen approaching me at a determined rate.

I have no fear of cattle, and an ox, like a steer, is a "fixed" bull and being handled daily is usually very gentle; but these looked and were so enormous that I felt a mild apprehension. I need not have. They lumbered up to me like a couple of friendly behemoths, and while one blew in my ear the other licked the sweat off my neck. They accompanied me to the fence behind the barn and remained there while I walked around to the front of the house to where a couple of women were talking to Oscar. I think it was Oscar. Anyway, it was the brother who never wore a shirt in summer and who boasted an abdomen as rotund as that of one of his "bulls." He was doing what he always did when there were lady visitors, presenting them with four-leaved clovers. I never discovered how he was able to do it, but in the middle of a conversation he could bend over (not easy for him) and pick out of what passed for a lawn a lucky clover to offer to his guest. If there was more than one guest he would find more than one clover.

I suppose you wonder what the foregoing has to do with the Tenth Commandment. Well, I envied the Howe boys their oxen, even though I would not have known what to do with them had I owned them, and I coveted Oscar's clover. I have not discovered more than half a dozen four-leaved clovers in my whole life, and I knew from Oscar's smile how it amused and rewarded him to be able to perform this little trick. I give things to visitors to my garden, too, but I am sure he got more pleasure out of his gift of a good-luck clover leaf than I do out of giving a slip of something with a botanical name a foot long. He was closer to the natural man than I, but I keep trying.

On our way home from Pennsylvania recently we stopped to visit and lunch with a lady who had gone around our garden last summer. I had not known her before, but we had mutual friends who guided us to her house 1,500 feet up in the Berkshire hills. We arrived in the middle of a perfect fall day. The sun was bright, and the air as crisp as a Winesap apple, as it should be in October.

We sat before a fire in a lovely old pine-paneled room drinking our pre-luncheon sherry, and we could see out of the windows a wide sweep of hills clad in late autumn colors of russet and gold. Far down the valley were a few open fields, a white church steeple, and a cluster of farms. I found myself sinning once more. I coveted the view—but soon realized that I was possessed of it as much as was my hostess. I took it with me when I left and have only to shut my eyes to see it again. I can add it to my own daily scene of ten miles of blue water with Western Mountain as a backdrop. I coveted her lavender plants also, and like a true gardener she gave me some, for gardeners are ever generous. Then, as I turned to take a last look across the rolling, wooded hills, a bluebird that was perched on a nearby bush lifted with a beat of wings and a flash of color and floated down the valley. What was it that Thoreau said? "The bluebird carries the sky on his back."

The First Domesticated Fruit

Any observant person riding the country roads in autumn cannot fail to notice, here and there, an apple tree bearing more than one variety of fruit. Usually it will be seen in a dooryard, or what at one time had been a dooryard, or in any event not far from one. I know of a dozen such trees, two of them on my own place and others where one would never suspect there had ever been a house—except for a crumbling hole in the ground and a lilac or two.

Years ago it was a favorite pastime of farmers, or even of those who had only a house lot, to graft one or two of the wild apples that volunteer in every uncultivated field or hedgerow. The scions would have been obtained from a neighbor's Baldwin or "Mac" or Red Astrachan, or even from some other wild tree on the place that bore worthwhile fruit.

After the grafts were set they were not usually given much attention, but in spite of that they soon provided a few bushels of apples that cost nothing but the picking, and helped stretch the family budget.

Not many people grow their own apples now, preferring to buy them from the supermarket. The fruit they buy may have fewer blemishes and may be more colorful, but it won't taste any better and is not likely to keep as well.

One of my trees is close by the bend of the road and just missed being bulldozed away when I dug a small pond alongside the barn. I am glad it escaped because, even as neglected as it has been, it is still worth more than the pond, which has a hole in its bottom through which all the water runs every summer. I have another tree on the other side of the house, which bears a small red apple that I have not been able to identify, but the one by the road is a Baldwin, and I have a bushel of its yield in the cellar.

A couple of weeks ago I worked away happily all one afternoon cutting the wild wood out of my Baldwin. About half the tree was wild, the other half tame. That the Baldwins tasted better than the wild apples was to be expected, but what interested me was that the wild ones were wormy and badly blemished, while the cultivated ones growing right amidst them were, for the most part, free of disfigurement and without worms. I learned then that it was not just a matter of larger and tastier fruit that caused the original Baldwin to be propagated, but also its ability to resist disease and insect attack.

When I was chatting with old Roy Bowden, I asked him when he set the scions. He did not remember exactly but thought it was in the mid-1930s, so the graft is about forty years old. He must have made it low on a small tree that subsequently suckered, for the wild trunk and the graft grow up from the ground side by side. The tree looks a little cockeyed since I cut the wild part, but it will grow better and annual pruning will soon get it into shape.

There was a Red Astrachan, too, that Lena Bowden told me gave wonderful early apples for cooking. I never saw it, and I guess it got chopped down when the wild apples and alders and whatever across the road from the house were cleared so that we could see the bay.

Apples have been cultivated as far back as there is recorded history, and farther, for they have been found in prehistoric kitchen middens in Switzerland. They were the first domesticated fruits our ancestors brought from the Old World to the New. Most of the early varieties are now hard to obtain, but many of those we look upon as almost contemporary are older than we suppose. The Baldwin was discovered as a wild apple in 1793 by a man named Samuel Thompson while he was surveying the line of the Middlesex Canal in Massachusetts. The "Mac" was found in Ontario by John McIntosh in 1796, and the Northern Spy near Bloomfield in New York State in 1800.

Apart from the Golden Delicious and some of the Greenings, people won't buy apples today if they are not highly colored (never mind how they taste), and of course they don't care whether or not the fruit will keep, as they buy only a few apples at a time.

Nowadays, when apples are picked they are put into cold storage at a temperature near freezing and taken out in small lots to be sold before they turn soft, which they do pretty promptly when they hit a heated store. My Baldwins, down cellar, will still be crisp in February. Lena maintains they are best in March, "when they are a little mellow," but I like them to crack as I bite into them, and if the juice runs down my chin, that is all to the good.

Handsome Fowl

A couple of pheasants were working down the frosty hillside when I looked out this morning. They were what Gilbert White would have called handsome fowl, male birds in full plumage with the white ruff showing very distinctly. I could not see what they were feeding on; insects, I suppose, for they would walk a few feet and rustle about in the dead leaves and withered grass, then look up warily and move on. Cock birds don't associate so amicably in the spring, for then they each have their harem to protect and attend to.

There are a lot of pheasants around here in Pennsylvania. They feed in the shattered cornfields all winter. The mechanical corn pickers are economical of labor but wasteful of grain, so there is always a bountiful supply of missed and broken ears for the birds to feed upon. I wish we had more pheasants in Maine, but they are not woodland birds and there is little for them to live on when the once open fields have gone back to woods. As you go south into the open areas of New England they increase in number, and by the time you get to southern Pennsylvania, where I am writing this, they are commonplace.

Pheasants are interesting birds, as they rank in order of domesticity somewhere between chickens, to which they are related, and truly wild birds like grouse and quail. They can be bred easily in captivity but in a few months, if they are set free, can make their own living and become feral. It takes a little while, though, and if they are released and shot at within a few days (as they are on some of the so-called "game farms") you might as well be hunting a flock of domestic biddies. You would have to kick them up to get them into the air.

Pheasants have been game birds for a long time. The ring-necked pheasant, which is our common bird, is a native of Asia that was brought to Europe by the ancient Greeks and to England by the Romans. It is said to have reached the east coast of North America in 1790 and is, by now, thoroughly naturalized wherever it is able to pick up a living. Species other than the ring-necked are seldom seen outside an aviary, although I once saw a Golden pheasant on the loose in England. It was a beautiful bird with its crown and back golden and the under parts of its body crimson.

Where there are deserted fields going back to woodland, studded here and there with wild apples (and fields like these are to be found all over New England), the game bird par excellence is the ruffed grouse, locally known as a "patridge." Actually there are no partridges native to North America, although a few have been introduced. Perhaps some early settler from Europe whose ornithology was not too exact so named them, and the name stuck.

Last spring I found the nest of a grouse at the foot of a spruce among the alders below my shore pasture, and so far as I know she brought off her brood. They stick together for a year, which is why one so often puts up several grouse in a covey. They usually break cover erratically, giving the hunter more than one shot if he doesn't get diverted.

At Amen Farm we have grouse around all winter, feeding on the shriveled wild apples. They seem to find food enough even in really tough winters, as they eat seeds, buds, berries, and insects impartially. They are very fond of the berries of the Russian olive, but the berries are usually gone before winter.

In northern Maine, in fact in all the wild parts of northern New England, the so-called spruce partridge is a common bird. In the Rangeley area I have seen four or five or them roosting on the limb of a spruce tree looking for all the world like Plymouth Rock hens. They are quite tame and will sit and let you knock them on the head if you have a mind to. I never have nor do I expect to, for I am told they taste like the spruce buds they feed on.

A good dog enhances the pleasure of grouse shooting, for without a dog to point the birds you are not likely to know where they are until you almost step on them—and then they will take off with a whirr of wings, startling even the most experienced hunters. It does not take many seconds for a grouse to put a lot of twigs and trees between it and a gun.

My Brittany spaniel, Quince, likes to go out with me, but he is not much help because he is as old as I am and set in his ways. He has never been properly trained (my fault), and hunts so far ahead that any birds he puts up are out of range. It makes no difference, though. A walk with a faithful dog in a thinning woodland with the leaves crisp underfoot is its own reward. Birds are only a bonus.

Moonshine

When I took Quince out for his prebedtime stroll last night, a full moon was fading in and out of the low-hanging clouds driving in from the southwest. Though it was for the most part obscured, the night was well-lighted and I could see the top of the hill a mile down the road where, by the cemetery, it dips in a steady decline to Naskeag Harbor.

Moonlight is not as important to us in the twentieth century as it was to our forebears who had no automobiles or electric lights and who planned their nighttime excursions to coincide with the phases of the moon. I am sure Jane Austen enthusiasts will recall her references to visiting around on moonlit nights, the only nights when dinner parties and balls were planned. While this must seem an infinity of time ago to the youth of today, who have grown up with all the disadvantages of "progress," it was well understood by my parents. Even I can remember, as a child, when I had fallen downstairs and broken an arm, being conveyed to the country doctor's office behind a horse. The only lights on the vehicle were carriage lamps lit by large candles with reflectors behind them that cast a feeble beam ahead. Certainly they were not bright enough to light a country road on a dark night. I have just such a trap in my barn now, which needs a quiet old mare about fourteen hands and broken to harness. I don't suppose that cobs are bred today, not in this country anyway, but they were the type of horse used in traps and governess carts when I was a child. They were close-coupled, so to speak, being a little shorter fore and aft than saddle horses and quite rotund in conformation.

While the astronauts have shattered some of our most cherished ideas about the moon, without any material compensation as far as I can see, they have not been able to make much impression on lunar folklore. People go around turning their silver over at the sight of a new moon (although a lot of them don't know whether they are looking at a new moon or an old one in its last phase), and the lovelorn still get goosebumps on moonlit nights. I suppose there are some who believe that if you fall asleep with the moon shining on your face you will wake up with it twisted out of shape. As my bedroom faces north, I can't testify.

One of the most indestructible pieces of moonshine is the belief that the moon is responsible for frost. I will admit that some things point in the direction of the moon's complicity, but that merely illustrates why the courts are so reluctant to hang men on circumstantial evidence. In our part of the world cold air, as anyone knows who has studied daily weather maps, moves in from the great continental land mass to the west, just as in Europe it drifts in from the vast Russian steppes to the east. Warm air comes from the

56

east in North America and from the west in Europe, in both cases being laden with moisture from the ocean, and accompanied by clouds. Frost rarely occurs on cloudy nights because the clouds, filled with moisture, blanket the earth, holding in the heat. Though we may not see the moon because of fog or low clouds, it is just as full above them as it is farther inland, where my neighbor's garden is devastated. Here at Amen Farm we rarely get a killing frost until toward the end of October, and one year it was the tenth of November. The factors that bring frost are a center of high barometric pressure accompanied by cold air moving in from the west, and the clear skies that these great high-pressure cells bring with them as they move across the country.

As a full moon is just about the most conspicuous object in the landscape on a clear night, it is easy to associate it with frost, but it is only an innocent bystander, and plenty of killing frosts occur when only the ghost of the full moon is seen in the new moon's arms.

I have seen a full moon shimmering on the waters of Acapulco Bay, but it did not seem to have any influence on the temperature. Maybe tropical moons are meant for love and not for gardening.

Wreathing

This is a dark morning and a warm one, warm for Maine in mid-November, that is, and there is no hint of Thanksgiving or Christmas in the air. Nevertheless, in spite of the mildness of the day, I know the holidays will before long be upon us, because I just saw a high-sided truck piled with greenery go lurching along the road.

Around here, wreathing (making the basic undecorated Christmas wreath) is an annual event as predictable as the arrival of smelt in Surry Bay in December or alewives fighting their way up the brooks in the spring. Wreathing starts about mid-November, and by early December there is hardly a dooryard that does not have a few piles of wreaths ready for the dealer's truck to carry away. Some go to local florists to be embellished by the addition of cones and berries and reindeer moss, while others are shipped south to be sold and decorated locally.

The preferred material for a solid long-lasting wreath is fir. It is softer than spruce and it exudes that haunting deep-woods fragrance of balsam. We send a few Christmas wreaths every year to friends who live far away, and when they write their thank-you notes they never fail to comment on the heavenly fragrance that enveloped them when the box was opened.

While wreathing is hard work, particularly if there has been a fall of snow before the "brush" has been gathered from the woods, it is an undertaking that the wreathers enjoy, as well as one that provides them with extra money for Christmas presents or more essential items, such as children's winter boots and sweaters. It has always seemed to me that after wreathing time all the kids break out into a kaleidoscope of colored sweaters, running heavily to the greens and reds.

Brushing is probably the hardest part of the job; it consists of gathering the "tips" that are woven into the wreaths. There are different ways of accomplishing it. If it is a big operation and the material is being gathered from the wreather's own land, a truck or woods trailer may be loaded with whole branches which are taken home and stripped. For the more modest household, the branches are tipped as they grow in the tree and are collected in bags and lugged out to a car or truck. There are usually people who ask permission to brush on my land, and I have found that on the whole they are careful and do no damage. If the job is done properly it may even shape up smaller firs being grown for Christmas trees; and for those whose future lies in the pulp mill, the loss of a few lower branches is all to the good.

Wreathing is essentially a family operation, although there is hardly a house where the women do not make a few wreaths even if the menfolk don't assist. A few family operations are "big time." I know one where the combined effort generated an income of $3,500. That represents a lot of wreaths at $26 a dozen for sixteen-inchers and $40 for the twenty-four-inch size, which seems to be the going rate for the basic undecorated wreath. But $3,500 is a high figure. Somewhere in the neighborhood of $1,000 for a family's Christmas wreathing would be a fair average. Even that is a substantial addition to the family income.

The making of wreaths is done wherever space is available, in the house, the shed, or the cellar. As soon as they are made they are placed outdoors so that the needles, called "spills" locally, won't fall off. It is thought that a touch of frost before the tips are gathered glues them on a little more firmly. Inevitably, in working with the brush, spills do fall off, and one of my local friends told me she didn't get the last of them out of the house until spring. While making wreaths is fun and profitable, it is hard on the hands; I do not recommend it to city ladies with polished fingernails.

If you find some discrepancy between $26 a dozen for sixteen-inch wreaths and what you pay for a single decorated wreath, it is in the cost of the decorations, the labor involved in applying them, the packaging and mailing costs—and profit. All I can suggest as an alternative is that you come to Maine and make your own.

The Pure in Spirit

Where I live I am within radio reception of a local station that runs a continuous weather summary and forecast. It operates on what it says is a frequency of 162.4 megahertz, which does not mean much to me since all I know about electricity is the difference between watts and volts, and I am not too sure of that. The forecast is divided into reports and predictions for several inland areas, but it is not until these are disposed of and the marine forecast is aired that I prick up my ears. From where I sit I can see the Atlantic Ocean or, it would be more accurate to say, I sometimes can—because now is one of the times it is not visible. The U.S. Coast Guard Station on Matinicus Rock has just reported wind gusting to sixty-five knots with zero visibility. Farther to the eastward much the same conditions prevail and, as I live midway down the coast, I can't see any better. I can see my sheep, a couple of hundred yards downhill in the shore pasture, but that is about all.

I really don't know why I keep sheep. I don't have enough of them so that they pay their board, even though one does appear, occasionally, as

lamb chops. I also have a sweater my wife made for me from the unbleached wool of one old ewe. It still smells of lanolin, an odor I find pleasant and sort of homesteady; but despite the benefits of chops and sweater I still have to feed out hay, which is expensive—for hay is not, as many people seem to think, that stuff that grows by God's gift in an old deserted field. I have had a good many people, who just wanted their fields mowed, offer me the "hay" as a gift; they did not understand when I declined their generosity. Hay is like any other crop. The land has to be cultivated, limed (probably), and fertilized one way or another. The grass seed and/or alfalfa or clover or whatever, has to be planted. The hay has to be cut at the right time to obtain the most nourishing crop, and it has to be made, baled, and stored. Then it may rain for a week while your hay is down. It is no longer popular to blame it on the Lord's will and bite the bullet, but whether you call it punishment for your sins or bad luck, the result is the same—no hay.

The rain is coming in flat-on now, riding, I would guess, about a thirty-knot breeze. I say breeze though most folks would call it a gale, because I grew up at sea, and on the Beaufort scale thirty knots is not a gale, though it is close. Anyway, it has kicked up enough sea so I am glad the offshore islands scattered to the eastward, Pond Island nearby, and Placenta and Great and Little Gott farther out, break up the long send of the Atlantic swells that would, otherwise, soon tear up my shoreline. This is not the placid robin's-egg blue ocean the tourists admire.

The sheep are now standing near some boulders and ledge that shoulders up through the thin soil, and in the scuds of rain it is difficult to distinguish sheep from rocks. They are standing there by preference, of their own free will, and I would like all those who bugged me last winter for leaving them out in the weather to so observe. I just couldn't stand being cast in the role of a candidate for prosecution by the S.P.C.A. for another season, so I had Carlton Gray come down and knock together a shelter for them. I don't have his bill yet, but even though Carlton is a mighty moderate man in his charges (unlike other builders I have known away from Maine), I am pretty sure the amount will be more than it would have cost me to buy half a dozen lambs on the hoof. So, to go back to the beginning, I really don't know why I keep sheep. I guess, perhaps, it is because I was raised in an Edwardian ambience where little white lambs stood for the pure in spirit, and I have always recognized the wisdom of keeping a little pure spirit around, particularly with the Christmas season almost upon us.

I know there are a lot of nice things about Christmas. What I like best is the nostalgia it generates. I like to remember Christmas past; I am not very keen on Christmas present. Too much of it seems to be involved with giving and receiving. Material things, that is. It is true that for a couple of days people appear more concerned and kindly than usual, but it does not last. By the time they are over their New Year's hangover their principal concern is how to pay for the Christmas bender. I feel like my ancient friend (now long gone) Gertrude Jekyll, who said, "Forgive us our Christmases as we forgive those who Christmas against us." She hated, particularly, the exchanging of Christmas cards by people between whom there was not really any affection or regard.

As for me, I love to hear from my real friends. (They don't have to be old friends; sometimes someone new will strike such a deep chord of understanding, what the Spanish call *simpatia,* a feeling more enveloping than the English word "sympathy," that I ask, "Why did I have to grow so old before I met you?") As for the others, I feel obliged to them but I would say, as Shakespeare said, "Sweet friend, for Jesus' sake forbear."

Alas . . .
the fleeting years
slip by

HORACE

A Scene Done in Charcoal

Snow fell thinly most of yesterday. There were occasional gleams of watery sunshine, but black clouds were soon driven across the bright spots and the snow drifted down. The day before had been one of high winds and lashing rain, and the thermometer had been rising and falling like an elevator. This morning dawned clear and still, so, accompanied by Quince, I set off to see what the outside world looked like.

Butterscotch may not be around when we start out, but we don't get far, Quince and I, before there is a pattering of feet and she passes us at a gallop, to wait until we catch up. I have never been able to discover why a cat that is so agile and light on her feet sounds like a racehorse crossing a covered bridge when she passes you. We wandered on into the woods and Butterscotch followed for a while, but she suddenly decided to climb into a small spruce tree, and there we left her. She tires easily or gets bored, and after she has had enough, asks to be carried. As she weighs almost twelve pounds, I don't do any carrying until we are on the way home, and today we were headed out, not in. I suspect she thinks herself still a kitten, like some ladies I know.

The sun was shining "outside" but it was dark in the woods. Not black, but gray—a scene done in charcoal. There was about half an inch of snow underfoot, and the floor of the forest was a crazy pattern of small fallen branches and roots, showing dark against a white background. I had not realized how tree roots pattern the floor of a forest nor how many of them there are. When the ground is bare they are all much the same color as the earth, and when it is snow covered you can't see them at all, but with just a minimum of white they stand out in startling contrast.

Although the bird feeder has been filled with evening grosbeaks, goldfinches, pine siskins, chickadees, and occasional blue jays and cowbirds all week, there were none of them in the woods today except, of course, the inevitable chickadee that followed us along chanting his cheerful little name call. On one trail there were tracks of snowshoe rabbits or, more correctly, hares, but there was no saying whether there had been one or a dozen of them, for they twisted and doubled back upon themselves repeatedly. A fox had walked daintily across a clearing, followed the trail awhile, and then jumped off into the underbrush. His track just stopped as though he had vanished into thin air. Perhaps he was after the hare.

When I took the lane downhill to the shore, I was surprised to find the old hackmatack that has spread its dead branches like a skeleton against the sky for as long as I have lived here lying prone in an alder thicket. I am glad it did no damage in its passing but I am sorry to see it go. It was a big open-grown tree and was a great favorite with the birds. Years ago the ospreys perched on its topmost branches where they could watch the gulls and steal their fish, but they are rare now—killed by pesticides. In recent years, since the tree died, it has been a favorite gathering place of crows, an occasional raven, and great flocks of grackles looking like some strange black fruit on its branches.

It was my fault that the hackmatack succumbed. When the shore road was made, the spoil was bulldozed over its roots. I knew it would be killed but everybody said, "You can't kill a big hackmatack with a little dirt." And I, knowing I was wrong to do so, allowed myself to be persuaded. I guess we acquire a lot of our problems that way.

Halfway back to the house I heard a plaintive meow, and there was Butterscotch laboring up the hill behind us. She had probably been sitting comfortably in her spruce tree while Quince and I were ducking around blow-downs but, when we passed her on the way home, decided to follow us. She came plowing up through half an inch of snow looking like an exhausted Arctic explorer with his igloo just in sight.

Yes, I carried her a few hundred yards, and it was uphill too, but she rewarded me by massaging my shoulder and purring in my ear.

The Edge of the Blade

When I opened my eyes this morning the room was chilly and I noticed that the friendly glow of the light in the electric clock was absent. Outside, the shutters were banging and a sleety snow was driving against the hillside. I was in a very convenient house, "all electric," but without power—as now—I was suddenly back to 1700 when the house was built.

I kindled a fire in the big open fireplace but we could make no coffee because we have no pot to use on an open fire. We have no water either, as that is pumped electrically; for the same reason we cannot flush the toilet more that once. Had we not, on the wall, a hundred-year-old pendulum clock we would not know the time. The stove is electric, so we ate cold cereal for breakfast. If my wife had been taken with a desire to clean the house she would have been unable to do so: an electric vacuum cleaner is an odd looking and useless object without its familiar hum. There was hot water in the electric heater tank but no way to get it. The little man in the refrigerator stopped making ice cubes, too, but I didn't want ice cubes anyway. There were, of course, no lights—and they would have been especially welcome on so dark and stormy a morning.

My wife and I sat bundled in front of the fire, spooning up our cold cereal and pondering the thinness of the blade edge on which our modern civilization balances. We were in Pennsylvania, but we would have been better off at home in Maine, for there we cook with bottled gas and have an emergency generator to provide power. But for how long—a couple of days, a week perhaps? Then what?

The fact of the matter is that so long as all the intricate machinery of modern life meshes as it is supposed to, all is well, but if it hiccoughs a couple of times we are right back where we were two centuries ago, with neither the equipment nor the skill to use it that our ancestors possessed. In the event of a really major breakdown lasting for more than a short period, the only people who would be able to survive would be those who we now consider underprivileged members of backward rural areas, the ones who cook and heat with wood, who draw water from a well and use an outhouse. The aristocracy of that new world would be my Pennsylvania Dutch friends who drive along the roads in little black carriages and turn into farm roads that spurn the poles and wires of the utility companies. Their neat houses and enormous barns stand as they have for 200 years, sheltering strong men and sturdy women and apple-cheeked children, as well as cattle and horses—and the yield of the fields and gardens sufficient to feed all of them.

The next time you hear some pot-valiant patriot talking about "We should drop a bomb and go in and clean things up," give a thought to that knife edge.

Peace Within

Today, through universal travel, instant communication, and the psychic wisdom of news analysts who know everything as soon as it happens (and some things that never happen at all), we are becoming one with the legendary professor who knew more and more about less and less until finally he knew everything about nothing.

Being a countryman, and thus a little removed from events that are loud but unimportant, it appears to me that all of us would be better off if we tuned out some of the world's chatter and did more thinking of our own. A good place to begin would be at home. It would help if, after listening to a speech by some prominent person, we immediately turned off the television set. We would thus avoid the comments of a battery of "experts" who, within seconds, tell us what it was we heard or, anyway, their version of it. They are as entitled to their opinions as we are to ours, but being introduced as interpreters, and having the last word (since the speaker has no opportunity of rebuttal), they are cloaked with an aura of wisdom far more profound than they possess.

For a long time we have been told that this is one world, and we are assailed hour by hour, almost minute by minute, by stories of momentous events and enormous undertakings, usually unpleasant, occurring in it. Somehow or other the idea that only gigantic enterprises are important has gained general acceptance, so we forget that the whole, no matter how stupendous, is no larger than the aggregate of its parts. This attitude is fostered by news analysts who read profound and earth shattering meaning into events—perhaps interesting, but really unimportant—that will have vanished into the unregretted past by the next day. This is particularly true of the reporting of political events where sleuths, not only of both major parties but of all the bureaucratic kingdoms and principalities, listen each night outside each other's bedroom doors. If they hear a sneeze, or the toilet being flushed, it is reported the next morning as proof that someone's worst predictions are about to be fulfilled.

It is inevitable that a constant preoccupation with great events (or, anyway, events that appear to be great at the time) and problems over which, by their very nature, we can have little influence, dulls our appreciation of smaller matters, ones that we *can* be a part of, ones that in reality make up a happy life.

Henry Thoreau said, "I have traveled a good deal in Concord." But out of those small domestic journeyings, accompanied for the most part only by his own thoughts, he constructed a philosophy that enabled him to reply to a fool who asked him when he was dying if he had made his peace with God, that he had not known that they had ever quarreled!

Gilbert White, who lived all his life in a small village (he remarked that it consisted of "one single straggling street, three quarters of a mile in length"), left to the world a lasting legacy of rural peace within the covers of *The Natural History of Selborne*. He did this during the period of the Napoleonic Wars, and was, of course, aware of them like everyone else at that time, but he did not permit this knowledge to breach the walls of his intellectual life. All but a few of the leaders of those wars are long forgotten, but Gilbert White's memory lives on, and men still live in spirit with him in his peaceful undertakings.

In our own time, men like Hal Borland, Joseph Wood Krutch, Eliot Porter, Loren Eiseley, H. J. Massingham, my neighbor E. B. White, Henry

Beston (whose *Northern Farm* should be on the bookshelf of all men who love the country), and many others have, each in his own way, shown that the very underpinnings of life, things that are universal in appeal, are the small daily felicities that are a part of even the meanest existence.

I do not suggest these men were, or are, unaware of or unconcerned with the tragedies of their times. Though he built his philosophy around the life of a small New England town, no one was more outspoken in his opposition to slavery than Henry Thoreau. Robert Frost's poetry is overflowing with the beauty of small country sights and sounds, but only a deaf man could fail to hear the deeper meaning.

No matter how the storm rages without, there can be, if we will it, peace within. Happiness depends in no mean measure on our ability to gain pleasure out of small things. We may be grateful that a war is ended, or a dictatorship overthrown, but happiness comes from discovering the first crocus or smelling the fragrance of apple pie in the kitchen. I am glad that, after many years, we have resumed relations with the Chinese people (although like Thoreau with God, I had never quarreled with them), but I am not happy about it in the same personal way that I am about the pussy willows I just found blooming in a ditch across the road from my barn.

"Is There Honey Still for Tea"

When my English friends speak of fixtures they are not thinking of devices fastened to walls to hold lights, but of some arrangement or appointment that has been made definite. In our house tea is a fixture. I do not mean the tea itself, but the meal, the social custom that revolves around drinking tea, for the institution of "teatime" far transcends what one drinks—although, on second thought, I doubt any substitute would create the same mystique.

I suppose tea is important to me because I went to England early enough in my childhood to become thoroughly indoctrinated. The Roman Catholic church is alleged to maintain that if it has the education of a child until it is seven, the Catholic stigmata are permanently imprinted on its psyche. I suppose the same principle applies to tea drinking.

Samuel Pepys records in his diary in the year 1660, "I did send for a cup of tee (a China drink) of which I had never drank before," but tea did not assume the character of a national religion until a good deal later—perhaps the early nineteenth century. We Americans are dedicated coffee drinkers, although it is interesting to note that we were tea addicts (at the time of the Boston Tea Party) when the English favored coffee. Times have changed, though, and now the English drink about twenty times as much tea as coffee and we use twenty times as much coffee as tea.

In America heavy users of coffee—truck drivers, who want to stay awake, and in fact all people engaged in hard physical work—think of tea as a "sissy" drink. If they were to drink it as English workmen do, or as it was served to me by English soldiers during the war, they would soon change their minds. Tea, scalding hot, well laced with sugar and milk, and so strong it would melt the quills on a porcupine, is a drink it takes courage to contend with.

Part of our disillusion with tea is the fault of roadside restaurants. If they served coffee as badly made as is their tea, their customers would throw it at them. To begin with they should use about twice as much tea as is contained in the average teabag; the cup should be hot; and the water boiling vigorously. Of course tea should not be made in a cup to begin with. What is needed is a good-sized heavy teapot, but I am not expecting perfection in a roadside restaurant. It is only since glass percolators came into being that roadside coffee is potable. There must be a few readers old enough to remember when restaurant coffee was made in large "silver" gas-fired urns behind the counter, urns that bubbled contentedly along from the time the place opened in the morning until its doors were shut at midnight. The first cup of freshly made coffee was vile, because the inside of the urn was coated with rancid coffee oil, but those that were dispensed later were appalling.

Checking on the figures for coffee vs. tea consumption, I ran across a piece of interesting information. It is nothing that is going to make money either for me or for you (which seems to be the criterion of education these days), but I was interested to learn that three Americans made part of their fortunes in the tea trade. They were John Jacob Astor, Thomas Handasyd Perkins, and Stephen Girard. I am particularly interested in Stephen Girard because when I lived near Philadelphia I kept my pennies in the Girard Trust Company and observed that on a landing on the stair to the safety deposit vault stood Stephen Girard's desk. It was dark with age and quite roughly made. It looked like the sort of thing a cellar craftsman would knock together. A modern banker would be ashamed to own it, but it served its purpose and proved it is the man and not the equipment that is important.

Amen Farm teatime is four o'clock, which is about the time, in winter, when I am tired of doing whatever I have been at all day and need a break before I start to think about dinner. By four o'clock it is pitch dark anyway. In summer it is light until ten o'clock, but as I have been up since five I am ready to knock off. Yes, four o'clock is about the right time for tea; later it interferes with dinner and earlier you feel you should go back to work. Of course we have just tea and a cookie, and not a high or nursery tea where one sits at table and devours rolled watercress sandwiches, or flat cucumber ditto, cold ham, or a boiled egg, or what the English call "Thunder and Lightning," which is scones buttered and spread with strawberry jam topped with heavy clotted cream. I once tried to have tea served in my office but I had to give it up because everybody thought I was slightly mad—although I noticed they all drank coffee whenever they felt like it. It is just a matter of custom.

I think I like tea in winter best. I never sit down to it without being reminded of one of my favorite eighteenth-century authors, a poet actually, William Cowper, who in his immortal poem, "The Winter Evening," wrote:

> *Now stir the fire, and close the shutters fast,*
> *Let fall the curtains, wheel the sofa round,*
> *And, while the bubbling and loud-hissing urn*
> *Throws up a steamy column, and the cups,*
> *That cheer but not inebriate, wait on each,*
> *So let us welcome peaceful ev'ning in.*

I have visited Cowper's house in Olney several times, and the fireplace and the sofa are still there. It takes only the slightest stretch of the imagination to feel that Cowper is also somewhere along the back hall that leads toward the garden where he tended his tame hares. The dusty old curator looks, too, as though he is a neighbor of Cowper's in for a fragrant cup.

Tea, in England, was originally an upper-class social occasion, but soon was taken up and enjoyed by lesser folk. The lady who is supposed to have started afternoon tea was Anna, Duchess of Bedford, but nowadays everybody, upstairs or down, worships at the shrine of teatime. In the beginning of the eighteenth century the "quality" dined early, and it was not until dinner-time had slipped to the hour of seven that tea crept in as something to fill the void. The custom was well established in Jane Austen's day, as any confirmed Janeite knows.

Now, in April, I can again drink my tea by daylight and think of spring, which reminds me of another English poet, one of my own generation, who wrote:

> *All suddenly the wind comes soft,*
> *And Spring is here again;*
> *And the hawthorn quickens with buds of green,*
> *And my heart with buds of pain.*
>
> *My heart all Winter lay so numb,*
> *The earth so dead and frore,*
> *That I never thought the Spring would come,*
> *Or my heart wake any more.*

It was Rupert Brooke, of course, who also wrote a poem about Grantchester where he punted up the River Cam to tea. No one who has ever been there will forget:

> *. . . Oh! yet*
> *Stands the church clock at ten to three?*
> *And is there honey still for tea.*

Harbingers of Spring

William Wordsworth, who is not my favorite poet (although there are some odd couplets that I retain in my memory, such as "The Rainbow comes and goes, And lovely is the Rose") expressed one thought that came to me this morning when I was on my knees admiring a handful of crocuses thrusting toward the light through a bed of periwinkle. It is in the "Ode on

Intimations of Immortality," which Ralph Waldo Emerson praised so highly and which generations of reluctant school children have had to memorize. Wordsworth wrote:

> *There was a time when meadow, grove, and stream,*
> *The earth, and every common sight,*
> *To me did seem*
> *Appareled in celestial light,*
> *The glory and the freshness of a dream.*
> *It is not now as it hath been of yore . . .*
> *The things which I have seen I now can see no more.*

Now I am grown I survey crocuses and other humble flowers from an altitude about three times greater than I did as a child, so I thought if I went on my knees to them I might recapture the old magic and escape the "Shades of the prison-house [that] begin to close upon the growing boy." I was amazed at my success. Memories of my childhood came flooding back: the prim little beds bordering the path to our front door, which I recalled were covered with periwinkle, even as mine are today, and the small old-fashioned daffodils rising above the green leaves and purple flowers of the vinca.

I remembered, too, the bed along the fence, where the fat red buds of the peonies would be showing among last autumn's dead leaves, and the crocuses in a row as an edging (we did not know much about "naturalistic" planting in home gardens in those days) would be flaunting their yellow or purple or white or striped petals to the sun. We liked the big yellow ones best and held them under our friends' chins, as we did buttercups, to see if they liked butter. I still have them in my garden and they are as buttery as ever, though they are scattered here and there in clumps and no longer grow in rows.

All our crocuses in those days were Dutchmen. More sophisticated gardeners must have known about species crocus, but we were content with the same old favorites, year after year. We sometimes grew them in small pottery jars with holes in the side like strawberry jars, bringing them up from the cold cellar while snow was still on the ground and, after we had enjoyed them indoors, later planted them in the garden. After a period of convalescence, they rewarded us again for years.

I have crocuses now, from September till May, excepting only when the ground is snow covered. The autumn crocuses, which bloom in September, (those the old folks called "Naked Ladies" because the flowers emerge from the ground before the leaves) are now, in the spring, covering the ground under the lilacs with foliage as green as grass. It will die in mid-summer to be followed in September by lavender blossoms. *Crocus chrysanthus,* in a variety named Snow Bunting, has been trying to bloom every time the ground has been clear of snow since February. Farther south I have had them color the ground at Christmas.

Snowdrops are marvelously beautiful flowers when viewed from five inches instead of five feet. The three outer shell-like petals enclose the three inner ones that are green and white and frilled on the edges. For all their delicacy of appearance they are tough enough to be submerged time after time in ice and snow, to be beaten to the ground by heavy rain and torn by winter winds and still, after an hour or so of sunshine, look to all appearance as though they had just burst into flower. They take rather a long time to become established because the only time the bulbs can be bought is in the fall, and it has been my experience that not more than half survive the first winter. The best time to transplant snowdrops is while they are in bloom, so that if you are fortunate enough to have a friend who is willing to make the sacrifice, spring is the time to do it. Once they are well-settled they will spread, both by offsets and by self-seeding, so if you can be patient and are young enough, you can in five or ten years have a good showing. Some of mine came from Pennsylvania, where a friend dug a clump for me from beside a jump, in a field where horses exercised.

Most flowers of spring are small. It takes time and the heat of summer to mature things like roses and dahlias and hollyhocks. Outside my window grows a clump of tiny daffodils. They are perfectly formed, for all the world a miniature twin of a big King Alfred. There are six narrow petals less than half an inch long, and the crown is no more than a quarter of an inch across. The perfection of the blossom is amazing, but unless you kneel to it, all you see is a downcast yellow flower.

The pussy willows, too, bear close inspection; they are in bloom now, and the catkins of the alders are also pink in the swamps and meadowland. The amount of pollen shed by a single alder catkin is beyond belief. I do not know if any patient researcher has ever tried to count the grains of pollen—what my old friend Gilbert White used to call the farina—but the figure must be astronomical and is a good example of the prodigality of nature. If you want to test what I say, bring a branch of alder into the warmth of your house. You will spend all the next day brushing up the dust, as fine as the softest flour.

A House Called Tranquility

In a village not far from where I live, a narrow lane drops slowly down toward the bay. One side marks the boundary of a rough field, while the other is over-arched by a row of oaks growing along the old cemetery wall. At its entrance from the village street there stood for many years a small sign exhibiting the name of the owner and the single word "Tranquility."

As often as I have traveled that way it has cast a gentle spell upon me. I have always been curious about the low, grey-shingled house that stands facing the bay at the end of the lane, but I have never ventured into the entrance, for who would trespass upon the privacy of one who so quietly informs the world of his desire for seclusion? Although I know now who lives there I am still reluctant to enter, realizing that I could not in any event find at the end of that long path something that exists only in the mind.

Tranquility is more easily defined than achieved. Though one associates it with remoteness and solitude, the truth is that its dwelling place is in the innermost recesses of a man's soul, and it is the man who has already found tranquility who seeks the peace and stillness of solitude. Some circumstances and some surroundings are evocative of serenity, but unless one is attuned to its faint echoes it will always remain elusive.

I have learned over the years that there are books upon my library shelves that bring about a mood of tranquility. Both the words and the photographs in Rachel Carson's book *The Sense of Wonder* breathe untroubled orderliness: a picture of the silk bursting from a milkweed pod; a lonely, fog-shrouded figure bent against the sea wind; fallen leaves on an autumn pool.

Another volume that never fails me is *The Gentle People,* a book of pictures and prose about the Amish. One has but to meet them, if only through the pages of a book, to recognize that here are those who have made peace with the world. They are part of the land. They live, not by exploiting it, but in partnership with it, and the long irresistible passage of the seasons carries them on quietly all their lives, from spring to autumn, from summer to winter.

Then there is a volume, *The Quiet Eye,* given to me by a Quaker friend. Opposite a photograph of a fourth-century stone carving of the Nativity are Walt Whitman's words, "As to me, I know of nothing else but miracles."

Here on the coast of Maine, when the long streamers of fog drift in from the sea, sounds are hushed and surroundings become unfamiliar. Near at hand the mullein leaves, great woolly blankets, turn to silver as the mist collects upon them. The old lichen-covered apple trees drip small showers when a vagrant wind stirs the branches. In the distance the encircling spruces come and go as the fog lifts or falls. I have had visitors shiver and ask, "How can you live here? It would depress me." But there are others who say nothing; they just fade into the fog along the shore road and come back presently with their cheeks red, their eyes bright, and their spirits calm and whisper, "How wonderful."

Man has always had need of tranquility. His religions express this. All of them, one way or another, try to bring him peace. One day not long ago I drove up the Sheepscot River to the hamlet of Head Tide. I had not been there before and, seeing the white church crowning the steep hill, I climbed the stony path and peered in the dusty windows. There was no sound to be heard and no one to be seen. The rays of the afternoon sun cast shadows of the long windows across the white pews. I stood for a long time watching the motes dance in the sunbeams and allowing the stillness to flow around me. Presently a dog barked, the spell was broken, and I went on my way, but I carried with me a memory that together with others like it serves me well in time of need.

My neighbor's sign has added its mite to my store, and I think of it with gratitude. Of such small blessings is serenity compounded.

Uncle Henry

I was told yesterday that my neighbor, Uncle Henry Smith, was dead. He was really no kin, but the avuncular relationship is an elastic one and stretches beyond blood to include those for whom one has an especial esteem or respect. I had known him ever since I bought my place on Naskeag Point in 1957, and looked upon him as a part of the country, as I would a spruce tree or a granite ledge. He was a man of the land, strong, tough, and dependable.

He was, I think, the last man in the town who made his livelihood as a farmer. All his life, he had supported himself and a large family by the labor of his own hands. He had never eaten the bread of idleness, and he brought up his children to believe that it is a man's obligation to support himself.

Henry Smith's passing signifies not only the death of a man, but the erosion of a way of life and is thus doubly unfortunate. Ever more frequently men of his generation are taking their leave of us, and with them we lose a respect for independence and self-reliance that was intrinsic in their character.

The young men and women of today are as far removed from the life of Henry Smith's youth as they are from ancient Rome, and have as little understanding of it. When he was a boy there were neither automobiles nor airplanes; neither were there radios or television sets and, in the country, no electricity or telephones or mechanical refrigeration, and no paved roads. Eggemoggin Reach was never without a sail, not rich men's toys, but working vessels carrying on the business of the day. The coastwise steamers ran frequently and dependably, and on land trains were the accepted means of transportation. Over shorter distances, one rode a horse or drove a vehicle drawn by one, just as did the Romans, 2,000 years ago.

Far-reaching as these changes have been, others affecting society's judgment upon what were once thought to be fundamental virtues have been even more profound. At the end of the nineteenth century thrift, self-reliance, independence, and probity were the cornerstones upon which decent men built their lives. That some failed of accomplishment was regrettable but their failure merely served to illuminate the cogency of the basic principle. Today thrift is scorned; one must spend while money still has some value. Self-reliance is square; the government will take care of you. Independence is silly; one must be "with it." Probity is the greatest casualty. Judges and lawmakers must have written codes of ethics, so that they will know whether they are thieves or honest men.

One by one the leaves fall. More than the earthly remains of a self-reliant honest man lie in the stony ground of the old Naskeag cemetery, where the blueberries grow among the headstones.

Take Time to Stand and Stare

A good many years ago, Robert Louis Stevenson, in *A Child's Garden of Verses,* remarked that the world was so full of a number of things, he was sure we should all be as happy as kings. Aside from using a king's life as a criterion of happiness, an assumption that in this day is of dubious accuracy, the remark is essentially true. The difficulty is that most people past childhood go through life blind to all but their daily concerns and fail to see that multitude of things the world is filled with. Their happiness is built upon such uncertain and infrequent felicities as a new car or television set, the death of a rich aunt who has remembered them in her will, or a raise in pay enabling them to buy more, or newer, models of things they already own. I speak now of my fellow Americans, not of the millions in other parts

of the world who consider a square meal the ultimate in satisfaction.

I do not intend to convey the impression that I am an ascetic and scorn riches. I remember too well Samuel Johnson's comment that if poverty was not a very bad thing, so many people would not be trying to prove that one could live very well on a small income. What I do mean is that through neglect or habitual blindness, we generally fail to see the "number of things" that are at our hands every day, free for the taking. These are things that cost nothing in terms of money, which are constantly varied and renewed, and which, in one form or another, are always there for our pleasure if we will for a moment step out of the blinding mental routine we impose upon ourselves.

We do not need time or money to enjoy the wind or the stars or the rain or the thousand other constantly changing events that surround our lives, but what we must have is awareness and curiosity. All children are blessed with this state of mind; few of us retain it as we grow older.

The robins and our white rooster Rudy sounded the alarm for me this morning at first light, and since they seemed unlikely to turn it off, I got up and made a pot of coffee. The valley was brimming with a milky mist that reached midway up the long slope to the east. The air was still, and a hot day promised with the sun slowly burning off the haze. As I sat on a pile of boards, with my mug of coffee in my hand, I became conscious of a gentle movement along the weedy growth in front of me. I thought at first that a soft air was stirring the daisies, but as the sun became stronger the "flowers" turned into hundreds of white butterflies.

I recognized them as the "common white," not because I am a lepidopterist but because they are my enemies and lay eggs that hatch into green caterpillars that feed upon my cabbages. As I have no cabbages to worry about at the moment, I was free to enjoy the picture and to wonder why little clusters of white butterflies, four or five perhaps, would suddenly rise, gyrating into the air as though caught in a Lilliputian tornado. I don't know much about the sex life of butterflies, though I have read that bees rise into the empyrean to cohabit. If this is what the butterflies were up to, it strikes me as a singularly lovely undertaking, of a fairylike delicacy and charm. The entire performance was ended in half an hour, for as soon as the mist had risen all the actors dispersed and I went to my breakfast. I was glad I had taken time to stand and stare.

Property Lines

One of my city visitors, who was standing with me looking out of the library window onto the garden, and beyond to the fringe of mixed woodland that marks the end of the hayfield, asked, "Where is your property line?"

When I replied that I didn't rightly know he appeared surprised that a man wouldn't know where his property ended and his neighbor's began. He was conditioned by life in the suburbs, where everything is carefully divided and rigidly marked; where everything is neat and tidy and usually rectangular; and where, if your apple tree hangs over the boundary line, your neighbor is apt to cut it off, and the law supports him, although it won't let him keep the apples.

I suppose some day, if the population keeps increasing and the world stays the same size, both of which events seem probable, everybody will be boxed in, in such a manner. Around here property lines don't mean much to most of us, although I do know of one man who spent a lot of money and effort running a line through a patch of wild land, cutting out brush, and blazing trees. When he was done the line didn't come out where he thought it should, which distressed him considerably. If he had just relaxed and gone on assuming it was where he thought it was, he would have stayed content. That he didn't own the land wouldn't have made a bit of difference because he never did have any intention of doing anything with it. He told me the survey was off by sixty feet, and when I replied that I couldn't see that it made any difference since the ground wasn't worth anything anyway, he became annoyed and said that was not the point.

I think I know where one corner of my property is because the deed refers to a stone wall that comes onto the road near the house of my neighbor, Gordon Smith. However, by suburban arithmetic that is not a very accurate mark because the wall is more or less ten feet wide, about half the width of a city lot. I don't think that Gordon or I are going to get upset about where the law says we "abut." I can follow the wall back into the woods a few hundred yards but after a while it peters out, I guess where there were fewer rocks to be hauled off when the field was cleared. I have only the vaguest idea whose land I am on back there.

Some years ago I was chopping a little pulpwood and so was another neighbor. I was not sure of the boundary. He *thought* he knew but he wasn't positive either, so we just agreed to chop each side of a mutually agreeable invisible line. I don't believe either of us suffered much.

My line to the north'rd runs along Wallace Rockwell's property, not far from his shed where we used to scald and dress out pigs. (A friend of mine came along one night after dark, when the fires were blazing under the old oil drums we used to heat the water to get the bristles off the hogs, and said it looked like Dante's Inferno.) Anyway, neither Rocky nor I know just where the line is, and if we did we wouldn't waste our time or money marking it. If I know Rocky, he would rather go fishing, and so would I.

To the east I am hemmed in by the Atlantic Ocean, which is a rather formidable barrier, but if I trespass at low water and dig a few clams, the evidence of my larceny is erased by the next tide.

I have always enjoyed Walter Hard's story about the old Vermont native who, every time a piece of land that adjoined his came on the market, bought it whether it was any good or not. Finally, after he had purchased a particularly sorry piece of scrubby, rocky hillside, a neighbor asked him what he thought he was doing, buying up all outdoors. His reply was, "Don't like t'have folks ownin' land next t'mine. That's why."

Well, that's one way of owning all outdoors, but I have a better way and it doesn't cost anything. I just walk, and listen. What I take off the land is invisible. You can't prove damages when all that has been stolen is the fragrance of the balsams, the autumn fire of the maples, the scream of the blue jay, and the whisper of the wind in the pines.

Fruits of the Garden

One of the more pleasant tasks of late summer is the harvesting of the fruits of the garden.

In these days, when freezers are the rule, there is less canning than there used to be (although in my opinion tomatoes are better canned than frozen), but it is a poor countryman's kitchen that doesn't have some jars of jam on the shelves. We have the old standbys, strawberry, raspberry, currant (in a more elegant form called Bar-le-Duc) and gooseberry. Strawberry-rhubarb is not to be looked down upon either.

When I was a boy, people seemed to make more plum jam, and plum-and-apple jam, than they do nowadays. The apples stretched the less plentiful plums and assured the jam's setting by reason of the added pectin. Plum-and-apple jam was put up in large jars and was always on hand for small boys to slather thickly on bread, without making much of a dent on the contents of the larder.

Then, of course, there are pickles. Nobody yet has discovered how to freeze a cucumber successfully, and I hope they never do, so we pickle them: sweet, kosher, dill, whole, rounds, sliced. We pickle zucchini, too, and it is difficult to distinguish them from cucumbers.

There is also the dilly bean, which some inspired person invented a few years ago. At eighty cents a jar, which is the price they first sold for, I must have pitched about $200 worth of potential dilly beans on the compost heap last week. My personal preference in pickles is mustard chowchow that needs hard, crisp cauliflower to be perfect.

The potato haulms should be browned off by now and, if the spuds are dug and cured for a day or so before being stored in a cool cellar, they will keep well—provided the sprouts are rubbed off a few times during the winter. We never get many potatoes to store because I like to eat them when they are about half the size of a Ping-Pong ball, stealing them from the side of the rows before they have a chance to get large. Those that elude me are usually taken back to Delaware by my son-in-law, who says they are superior to the local irrigated product.

Peas, corn, and beans, of all species and varieties, we freeze aplenty. During my lifetime I have grown almost every variety of corn available, but have finally settled on "Wonderful," which I obtain from the Harris Seed Company. "Wonderful" is good both for eating off the cob and for freezing. We have a little device we got from the Vermont Country Store that splits the kernels and strips out the innards in one motion. I can recommend it to all who like cream style corn.

I learned years ago that onions grown from seed keep far better than those grown from sets. We are digging ours now and will cure them in the sun before we put them up attic to spend the winter. We were eating our last crop until May, which is pretty good going.

The garden also provides us with those aristocrats of the Allium family, shallots. We got our start from an old market in Washington, D.C., that has long since been torn down, though our shallots carry on from year to year. They grow in clusters rather like garlic; they also need curing, like regular onions, but this being done, will keep for years. The other member of the onion tribe we would not be without is the chive. We have a few clumps in the flower garden, and early, before the flowers appear, we cut the tender green spears to the ground, and chop and freeze them for later use on vichyssoise, or anywhere else we may desire.

The beets and carrots are ready to go to the cellar, and the various types of squash will be picked as soon as the stems harden. If you gather squash too soon, or if you fail to cure them before storing them, you will lose a lot. It should be remembered, too, that they ought to be handled like eggs and not like rocks. A small bruise on the skin will inevitably develop into a decayed spot on a squash.

Yesterday, when I was picking a pint of late strawberries, I noticed a splash of yellow amidst the broken cornstalks and found a couple of good-sized pumpkins. I suppose some people make pumpkin pie from scratch, but our cook uses the canned variety, so our pumpkins will be strictly for Halloween. With the roadside stands charging $2 or $3 apiece for them, it is worth poking a few seeds in the corn rows.

The Champagne of the Year

Well, it has happened again. The tourists, or most of them, are gone. The "summer people" are thinning out; the ones with kids in school left last week, though their elders may be around for a while longer.

The summer cottages are not yet boarded up. There is plenty of time for that before snow flies, and there is always a hope that a long weekend will allow a postseason visit, so let's not rush it.

Fishing lines with mummified worms glued onto rusty hooks sway in the wind from bent nails under deserted porches. Starfish, as brittle as cat ice, lie forgotten where they were put to dry in the sun. The first equinoctial blow will carry them off into the woods, along with the whitened clam shells, the faded blue mussels, and the odd scallop shells that had served as ash trays.

The last bunch of dusty goldenrod and wild aster can be seen through the cobwebby windows, where it was left on the center of the table, a relic of the final pick-up supper. On a bookshelf is an "arrangement" of driftwood and sand and British soldier moss and pebbles—pebbles that were so lustrous when they were fresh washed by the little waves lapping on the shore, but that now, like all things we clutch too closely, have lost their beauty.

The swallows are flown, all but one last brood, high in the barn rafters, their gaping mouths reaching over the edge of the nest to claim the food their parents have been swooping in arabesques to capture for them. They won't be around much longer either for, like the rest of the summer folk, they have business to attend to, miles from here. A fortnight ago they were as thick as flies on the barn roof, warming themselves in the first rays of the early morning sun; tomorrow they will be gone.

The next two months and more, before winter sets in, are the champagne of the year, and it is sad that our friends from away have to leave us. They will go back to crowded cities and busy suburbs, while we stay here and watch the world turn. Labor Day is not marked in large letters on the countryman's calendar. There is no color to be glimpsed in the woods yet. The fern fronds may be yellowing but the leaves of the trees hang dark and heavy. The fields that have been mown are green with the aftermath, and if there are cattle, they are grazing slowly across them. The gardens are rich with corn and squash and tomatoes and other delights that have been maturing all summer.

It will be six weeks before the woods take fire, and with any luck, six more before snow whispers down. We count the end of summer when autumn storms tear the flaming leaves from the maples and spread them like an old patchwork quilt under the naked trees. After that comes the hunter's moon. First will be the grouse rocketing up to put a thicket of alders in front of you before you can raise your gun to your shoulder. Later the whitetails that have been around all summer will suddenly disappear, and if you want to get "your" deer, you wander along back roads or tracks where the wild apples give off a heady fragrance as they lie beneath lichen-encrusted, broken old trees.

Foreign license plates become as rare as our own appeared to be during July and August. The drivers of the cars that pass raise their hands, or perhaps just their forefingers, from the wheel in recognition. Youngsters who stayed playing ball after the school bus left, thumb rides. You know most of them and where they live. All the kids wave, anyway. They have not been taught to be afraid.

The pace slows down. You can get in and out of shopping centers without waiting for a caravan of trailers, campers, and other bumper to bumper traffic to hesitate long enough for you to offer a quick prayer to St. Christopher before you stick your nose out. In summer you hoped that though the traveler's patron saint has been demoted, he still retained a little influence.

With apologies to Robert Herrick, we say, "Fair summer folk, we weep to see / You haste away so soon." But our tears are tempered by the knowledge that you will return again another year. Meanwhile, as a friend said to me the other day, "Roy, just think, in a couple more weeks we'll be able to park in the middle of the road again!"

Ongoing

Man, being the mathematical animal that he is, breaks down his years into months, weeks, and days; and his days into hours, minutes, and seconds. He speaks of the seasons: of spring, summer, autumn, and winter; and marks their arrival by the passage of the sun across the celestial equator. He has an overwhelming need to organize and classify, as though he was in an alien and hostile environment against which he must defend himself by being able to "computerize" and regiment the world about him. The days of his innocence, when he was one with nature, are past. They are gone irretrievably into the darkening years behind him. The future, too, is dark, because while knowledge can be accumulated, wisdom cannot.

Nature has no calendar. Daffodils do not open their blooms when the sun swings across the vernal equinox. The roses do not await the summer solstice to shake out their silken petals. Nor does the bluejay remain silent until the exact moment of autumn's birth to sound his harsh cry through the thinning woodland. The seasons are man's invention. Time and life flow ever onward like a river, without mark, or let or hindrance.

On the farm and in the garden we know only ongoing. Time flows year after year with the smooth inevitability of the tide, which each day floods in to cover the rocks and set swaying the seaweed that grows out beyond our shore pasture. The snow retreats; the grass in the meadow turns green, and then purple as the seed heads ripen, then to a faded olive as we make our hay. Lately I have watched the tall swaying plumes of the early golden-rod, *Solidago nemoralis,* transmuted from green through chartreuse into gold. Presently will come the purple of the ash and the flame of the swamp maple, and when they are past, the crisp leaves of the oaks will fade from bronze to brown, to rattle under the gusts of hail that precede winter's snow.

Plants, and animals other than man, do not measure their days and portion out their lives in driblets of time. They cannot think of their lives as short or long, but live them out as they are, and accept the sun and the wind and the rain, and the good and evil as it comes, without repining. The warbler that gasped out its little life in my hand after I had lifted it from the highway where it had been struck by a car, had lived all there was of its time. The lichens, dried and brittle on the boulder after a six-week drought, were transformed to orange parchment by this morning's shower, but had the rain not fallen, would have crumbled, by and by, into dust and nourished other lives.

Man no longer sees himself as a part of the world, as a contributor to and a partaker of its bounty, but as its owner and ruler. His interest in it is measured by how much he can get out of it, and if he is ever restrained in his plundering, it is because he has done something, the results of which have frightened him. We hear much today about air and water pollution and that something should be done about it. But little is really being done, and that only where man is afraid that if he does not mend his ways the results will be harmful to him. He has small concern with life other than his own. But the world, which was here through the long eons of time before his arrival, does not use his puny pendulum, and will be here long after he is gone.

Norman Douglas once wrote, "Men have lost sight of distant horizons. Nobody writes for humanity, for civilization; they write for their country, their sect; to amuse their friends or annoy their enemies."

That was not wholly true when he wrote it, though it was close enough to the truth that one could hear the whistle of the blade. It is not wholly true now, for there are men who are both learned and wise, which is a rare combination. The tragedy is that his plea, that we lift our eyes to those more distant horizons, is lost in the blast of war and the tumult of the cities.

Hunter's Moon

One of our local pedagogues recently acquired immortal fame by grounding a group of students who played hookey to go deer hunting during the opening days of November. I admire his courage but have doubts about his sagacity. You might just as well try to stop the natives of the state of Maine from digging clams at low tide, or from angling for trout when the black flies begin to bite, as to attempt to prevent them from trying to get "their" deer when the hunter's moon comes around.

Among the inalienable rights the Mainer believes to be his is the right to go into the woods in November and let fly at whatever he thinks is a deer. He is sure the only reason the matter is not specifically mentioned in the Declaration of Independence is because the document was written in the back room of a house on Market Street in Philadelphia, a big city. Mr. Jefferson was a country gentleman, who should have known better, but cities have a bad influence on people.

I myself am not a deer hunter. I have shot only one in my lifetime and that was from the kitchen window when I was about twelve years old. I was alone in the house when the deer walked out of the woods into our backyard. I got my father's old bolt action Mauser from the closet, slipped a cartridge into the breech, rested the barrel on the windowsill, took aim, and squeezed the trigger. There was a loud report and I was knocked over backwards. So was the deer—which was not surprising as it was only about 100 feet away. When my father came home he licked me, not for shooting the deer but for forgetting to open the window.

I do not post my property against hunters because I think that, like locking your house, it only keeps out honest men. Anyway, I have no objection to people walking across my land so long as they know how to behave themselves. I think posting land indicates an exaggerated sense of ownership and, since I read Robert Artrey's *African Genesis,* I am pretty scared of territorial rights.

I must confess I do not like to see cars bearing foreign license plates cruising slowly around with their bright lights on, just a little too late in the evening, but there is not much I can do about it. I followed one along the Bagaduce Road from Brooksville to North Brooksville a couple of days ago. The passenger sat with his gun half out the window, looking for something to shoot. He flicked a lighted cigarette out into the dry leaves alongside the road, and when I slowed down to see that it did not set fire to the countryside, he disappeared up a dirt road ahead of me.

I haven't seen many deer around this fall. There were only three in my back field all summer—a doe and twin fawns. The doe was gone before the season opened, and last night, about dusk, I heard three shots and saw someone run across the field and stoop and drag a white object about as large as my Brittany spaniel into the woods. I suppose there is only one of the twins left now.

Well, I've got my cows in the barnyard; to a city hunter a Guernsey would be a dead ringer for a big deer, and the black one might be mistaken for a bear. I don't let my dog out of the garden, but Butterscotch goeth whither he listeth, as is the nature of cats. However I don't think he has expended many of his nine lives yet. My own reserve has worn a little thin, though, so I shall observe the woodland from my window only, until "November's sky chill and drear" gives way to "bleak December."

Gilbert White's Barometer

Well, here it is the fourteenth of December, and I am trying to get my mind on writing. There are only eight more shopping days until Christmas, or at least there would have been under the old regime, but as Sunday is now discarded as a day of rest by many commercial types, I suppose there are ten. Anyhow, one is not reminded of New Year's.

A week ago a few flakes of snow, as big as white Leghorn feathers, drifted down to melt as soon as they landed, leaving no imprint. The grass is still green and more like mid-April than mid-December. During the night the wind shifted into the southwest and is now pushing sizeable whitecaps up the bay before it. The temperature is forty-two degrees and the barometer falling at 30.03; all in all, very un-Decemberlike.

I am possessed of two barometers. The one in my study is a little nickel-plated aneroid affair, actuated by the pressure of the atmosphere on a corrugated vacuum box. It looks very scientific, with a lot of tiny markings around the edge and part of its innards visible in the middle, but actually is not as reliable as the old mercury barometer that hangs in the living room. The old one was made in Hackney, then a suburb of London, by C. Lefever in the mid-1700s and, thus, is past its 200th birthday.

Mr. Lefever's instrument is just a glass tube of mercury mounted on a narrow vertical mahogany strip with a rectangular box on top where the barometric pressure may be read. The scale registers from 27.50 to 31.00, not quite so far in either direction as the aneroid; but as I am unlikely to witness either of these extremes, I am not concerned. I bought it in London many years ago, because it must resemble the instrument that Gilbert White records examining with such interest so regularly; and because I feel increasingly more comfortable in the eighteenth century than I do in the twentieth.

Like all old barometers, it supplements the scale with forthright statements. At 28.00 inches it says STORMY; at 29.00, RAIN; at 30.00, FAIR; and at 31.00, VERY DRY. One must not take these prophecies too literally because it is where the mercury is going, and not where it is, that counts. (Rather like politicians.) At the moment my barometer stands at FAIR, in spite of a gale out of the southwest and rain blowing in under the front door as though it were propelled by the slipstream of an airplane.

As Mr. Lefever was too wise to indulge in long-range forecasts, I am not going to make predictions about the coming year either, except to suggest that there will be rain and snow and sleet, that it will be hot and cold, windy and calm, and that no matter what it is, gardeners and farmers will complain.

New Year's is only something on the calendar, anyway. The tiny spears of the bulbous iris, *Iris reticulata,* whose flowers smell like violets, are even now pushing through the ground. They don't know anything about new years or old years either. They just continue to do what they have always done. We humans are the only living things that make a fuss about a new year. We tend to make a noise and stay up late and drink too much, but there is not anything really different about January first except we may have a hangover. None of our difficulties or problems are left behind; and, happily, none of the love and affection that others bear us is left behind either. It would be sad indeed if New Year's Day really did mean an end and a beginning. It won't for me, I know. I shall do as I always do when I come downstairs in the morning, push my spectacles back on my nose in order to get the right focus, squint at Gilbert White's barometer, tap it, and hope it says SET FAIR.

An Identity Problem

One of the problems facing the newcomer to a long-settled rural area like the coast of Maine is the duplication of surnames. It is difficult enough to couple up unfamiliar faces with different names, but when forty or fifty people rejoice in the name of Eaton, as for instance happens on Deer Isle, one is likely to throw up one's hands in despair.

In my own town of Brooklin, which the telephone company lumps together with Sedgwick, the directory lists eighteen Allens, eighteen Carters, and fifteen Grays, as well as a heavy seasoning of Smiths, Bridges, and Cousins. Interestingly enough, we have but three Eatons as against Deer Isle's forty-seven, and they have only three Allens to our eighteen. These are just the names listed in the telephone book, to which must be added all the uncles, aunts, cousins, nephews, nieces, and children living under the same roof; not to mention those who are fortunate enough, or wise enough, not to pay tribute to the New England Telephone and Telegraph Company.

The situation is further confused when two people with the same family name get married, as frequently occurs. The children produced by these alliances are thus double Eatons or Allens, or whatever the case may be, and have innumerable relatives of the same name on both the maternal and paternal sides of the family tree. As the "pill" was slow in getting to the coast of Maine, and winters are cold and long, families tend to be large.

There is also the fact that many people around here live to refute the

Biblical limit of threescore years and ten. Anyone who hangs up his clam hod before his seventy-fifth birthday is considered to have been stricken down in his prime.

The Brooklin Town Reports for the ten years ending 1969 list a total of ninety-three deaths. Of these, twenty-seven (or almost a third) were of people over eighty years of age, several being between ninety and 100. Of the remaining sixty-six more than a half—thirty-five—died between ages seventy and eighty. Statistically then, if you reside here, you have a 68 percent chance of living past seventy, and better than 37 percent odds that you will beat eighty. This is very comforting to those of us who are old enough to be thinking about our eventual dissolution, but it does not do a thing to help the stranger identify his neighbors.

About all one can do is stick to his home territory and learn a little of his lesson every week. I gave up on foreign parts when I said to a young man of my acquaintance on Deer Isle recently, "Hello, Marvin, how are you?" and he replied, smiling, "I'm not Marvin; he's my uncle." They are both high school age.

Clothes help a bit. There is an old chap around town who, as long as I have been here, is always seen in rubber boots turned down at the knee. They are as much a part of him as a limp is to another man. Clothing can fool you, though, because even here—in what the politicians are pleased to label a distressed area—a fellow can occasionally come by enough to buy himself a green plaid mackinaw to replace the red one you have become accustomed to.

Geography is a help, too. A friend stopped to look at my sheep. He said, "I didn't know you had any sheep." His tone was a little aggrieved, as though I had been concealing something from him.

I replied in a conciliatory tone, "I just got them," which of course prompted the question, "Where'd you get them?"

"From Wiggins," I said.

"Wiggins?" he queried. "I didn't know he had any sheep. I thought he just raised potatoes." Which is where geography came to my rescue. I was able to tell him that I meant the Benjamin River Wiggins, not the Sargentville Wiggins.

The only real solution is to be born in town. I am a little old to manage that but I am going to do the next best thing: I am going to be buried here. Come the resurrection I'll be starting even with a lot of other locals who won't know the people who were born after they passed on any better than I shall.

What is this life,
  if full of care
We have no time
  to stand and stare?

W. H. DAVIES

A Thin Blue Flame

One of the blessings of a New England winter is that it turns one inward. There is nothing like three feet of snow in your dooryard, and six inches of rutted ice on the roads, to make your fireside seem the most desirable place in the world. The geraniums on my windowsills are gay and cheerful winter companions which are never so bright as when they have a snowdrift for a background. Books that I have not had time to open all summer I can read now at my leisure, or dip into, flitting from one to another like a chickadee. If you like it, there is television, but any book in the house—even McGuffey's Third Grade Reader—will provide better fare.

Now, though hard cold lingers, the days begin to lengthen and it is almost six o'clock before we draw the draperies and turn on the lights, and by the same hour in the morning the sun is reflected from the snow onto my bedroom ceiling.

The world is never so blue as when it is snow covered. The sea is blue and the sky is blue; even the snowdrifts have a thin blue flame at their hearts. The patches of snow on Western Mountain are pale blue fields amidst the dark green of the spruces, but they change to pink or lavender in the sunset.

The birches do not reflect color. Their trunks are like chalk and are whiter in winter than at any other time of the year. They stand sharp against the miles of open water that separate us from Bass Harbor. They are broken and bent from last week's storm, some with their tresses still held fast by the snow at their feet, but they will shake off their bindings when the thaw comes and rise to sway again in the spring breezes.

The world I live in is incredibly lovely and peaceful. Even when the wind gusts the dry snow in great clouds around the corner of the barn, there is peace at the heart of it. There is no endless conflict here. One knows that when the storm has blown itself out, as it will in a day or so, the fields and woods will stretch as beautiful as ever, white and unsullied.

In a city and its suburbs winter is unpleasant and an annoyance. The streets are sloppy and dirty. The traffic, difficult at best, resolves itself into the most stupendous confusion at the slightest snowfall. I remember once, when I lived in the suburbs of a great city, spending from three o'clock in the afternoon until eleven at night negotiating the seven miles to my home. At that I didn't make it all the way, for I ran out of gas and had to abandon my car and fight the last mile on foot. The snowfall amounted to no more than three or four inches.

But the best of winter in the country and in its small towns is the increased sense of neighborliness that it engenders. Here the snow is soft and clean, there are no traffic jams, and on the rare occasions that a car gets into difficulty it is but a short while before someone stops to lend a hand. If there is a severe storm, neighbor telephones neighbor to learn if all is well. When the flashing light of the snow plow passes your house at night you know it is a neighbor, not just a social security number, at the wheel.

Death Comes to a Friend

One day last fall my wife and I had gone on our weekly shopping expedition, taking with us her little Brittany spaniel puppy, Happy. As I walked the pup around a bit, preparatory to returning home, a car parked alongside us and a man and a woman and two children got out. Of course they smiled at us, for few people can resist a puppy. The man, obviously a fisherman by his turned-down boots and heavy wool shirt, squatted and fondled Happy, who returned his affection by licking his chin. The woman and the children headed for the supermarket but the man stayed talking for a few minutes. When he got up to go, he said to me in his soft Maine voice: "I love dogs. I've got three, but the Lord didn't do right by dogs. He had no business having them die before we do. They don't live long enough."

I remembered that conversation when I had to make a decision about putting my old dog, Quince, to rest last week. He could have lived longer but was failing, so I did for him what I felt I had to do, and have been grief-stricken ever since. He had been in the animal hospital several times lately, and when I brought him home the last time he was feeling a little better physically, but his mind was affected as the result of an old trauma. He had taken to growling at people and would not obey anyone but me, although he was long-suffering with the puppy.

Quince and I had grown old together. Neither of us any longer had much enthusiasm for braving subzero temperatures to go walking over snow covered fields or on icy roads, so most of the time when I sat at my typewriter, he was content to lie at my feet. I know that he got more to eat than was good for him, but when he put his head on my knee and went through his act, saying as plainly as a dog could: "Please God [he was always a great flatterer], look down on your starving companion of many years and spare a morsel out of your plenty," I succumbed, as he knew I would.

I know that all the books on How to Raise Your Dog say that he must never be fed at the table; he must never be allowed to jump on anyone (just try to keep a puppy from doing so); he must never get on the furniture or upon your bed, and he must snap to attention and come running when you call. The fallacy of the book is revealed by its title. He is not *your* dog, you are *his* friend. If he has done you the honor of adopting you, it is as his companion for life, and he assumes that you have taken the same vow. He may be passing-pleasant to other people, but you are the center of his universe and the core of his love, and a dog's greatest need is to love and to be loved, as indeed it is the need of all mankind.

It was as his friend that I decided to play God, and to see that Quince passed from this world into the next as easily as possible. I lay awake all night seeking some other solution, if the truth be told, trying to avoid my responsibilities, but I could find no honorable way out—so in the morning, early, I told him what I had decided. He placed his fine broad head upon my knee and looked up at me with his hazel eyes now grown dim with age, and licked my hand. But when someone came to the door he growled, and the hair on his neck bristled, so I knew I had to go through with it. I told Albert Allen what I had decided and asked him if he would take Quince to the veterinarian for me. He nodded and said, "Yes, I know, he's been having a hard time lately." But I could see that he, too, was moved. So my friend has gone, by my hand, and the day is dark and I am desolate.

When I first tried to write this, tears blurred my eyes and I put my head on my hands and wept. Now, later, I can begin to remember the days of his youth when we wandered together along the shore and he chased the sanderlings, never catching one but pursuing them into the ocean until they skimmed off to alight again 100 yards ahead. I can recall our walks in the woods and in the fields, in the autumn, with the fragrance of the balsam almost overpowering. I can feel again the briars and the puckerbrush clutching at my legs, and Quince going into a perfect point, with his stub of a tail quivering and a forefoot lifted, only to discover that the "partridge" was a robin or even a butterfly. No, we were not mighty hunters before the Lord, Quince and I. The wild things had little to fear from us.

I grow old and I doubt that there will be room in my heart for another dog. My wife's puppy salutes me affectionately, and when Helen is not here, attaches herself to me, but when her mistress comes I am forgotten, which is as it should be. All I can do is add Quince to my memories. There was an earlier Quince that died young of a heart ailment; there was Lord Lancaster, a Scottie of distinguished lineage with the heart of a lion (we once had to take up the floor of the barn to coax him out after he had been there two days cornering a porcupine); there was Whiskey, a cross between a black Scottie and a white Sealyham, who died in my arms of distemper; and there were others, but all I can think of now is my friend, Quince.

This then is in the nature of a valedictory. I say in the nature of a valedictory because I hope it is not really a last farewell. Of one thing I am sure, that if there is a hereafter, Quince will be standing there sniffing all the shuffling feet crowding through the gate, hoping that the old familiar scent will at last arrive. There will be those who will pat his head and try to entice him away but, though he will politely wag his tail and perhaps even accept a bone, he will never give up his vigil. When I do arrive, if I ever do, he will forgive me for hastening his departure from this sad world where men live too long and dogs die too soon, and place his head on my knee once again and tell me that, no matter how long the wait, all is well now we are together again.

Domed Over by a Mouse

Rain fell, steadily and relentlessly, all day yesterday. One could literally see the frost coming out of the ground and the trees and shrubs absorbing the moisture. In just a few days of steady rain the color of the twigs of the deciduous trees begins to brighten, and the evergreens take on a liveliness, a living green, that has not been visible all winter. It is the recurrent miracle of spring that, no matter how often it has been experienced, remains still a miracle.

Spring does not appear with the vernal equinox and progress steadily onward. It takes two steps forward and a step backward, like a frightened puppy that wants to make friends but fears to overreach itself. One of the several books mined out of Henry David Thoreau's journals, and published posthumously, is called *Early Spring in Massachusetts.* In it Thoreau traces his wanderings through the woods, and by the shores of White's Pond, Walden Pond, and the Concord River, for which he used the Indian name Musquetaquid. He records the ice rotting in the ponds; the snow fretting away on the sunny side of the rock walls; the puddles that thaw and reflect a pale sun one day but freeze again the next. He tells of the purple horns of the skunk cabbages and the flood waters of the river carrying ice floes into the meadows. He is in search of spring, but records no overnight change. The transition, the annual resurrection, is accomplished little by little. We may think in May, when the leaves unfurl and extend, that we are witnessing spring, but what we are really seeing is the beginning of summer. Spring has been with us a long time.

With Thoreau by my side, I walked around my own pond this morning. We did not carry on much of a conversation. You don't talk to Henry, you listen; what talking there is, he does. He pointed out where a muskrat had its home in the bank. The entrance was not visible. It was under water, but its presence was betrayed by the remains of some water lily plants I had noticed were ravaged last autumn. I like muskrats when they build their mounds above the waters of a swamp, but I dislike them in a dam-breast, for they will, in time, surely destroy it. I shall have to lengthen the overflow pipe and raise the water level which will drown them out. Well, not really drown them, for they will just swim out and, I hope, depart for more convenient lodgings.

I pointed, diffidently, to a small nest in a young red maple and suggested it might be that of a goldfinch. It was quite tidy for a home that had survived the rain and snow and harsh winds of winter, so I examined it more closely and discovered it had been appropriated and domed over by a mouse. I was tempted to lift it from its foundation and roll it down the bank, for it was as round as a billiard ball and about the same size. The goldfinches stay around all year, and often build their nests in apple or maple trees, for they love to feed on the blossoms, first of the maples and then the apples. Thoreau often mentions goldfinches. They are friendly, happy neighbors, and will soon be donning their summer garments of yellow, or anyway, the gentlemen will. In Pennsylvania they are called salad birds by the old country people, from their habit of feasting on flower petals. As soon as you see the familiar golden balls swinging in arcs, pendulumlike, over your garden you know summer is at hand.

The fat knockwurst heads of the cattails along the bank at the shallow end of the pond are bursting and look as ragged, and about the same color, as the old ewe that I failed to get sheared last spring. I don't know how cattails travel, but I am sure if you were to dig a pond miles from any other water it would, in a year or so, be rimmed with them. I say I do not know how they travel, though that is not quite correct because I know that the seeds are carried by the wind like those of milkweed or dandelion, but it baffles me to understand how they are blown so far. The cattail, *Typha latifolia,* is found almost everywhere except in Australia (perhaps the seed could not blow quite that far) and a few parts of Africa and Asia, but otherwise the world is its dwelling place.

Away from the cities the pulse of the seasons throbs in a recognizable rhythm no matter where one may be. One countryman can understand another regardless of how far apart in the world they may live. They cultivate the same earth; the same rain that blesses the stony terrace of an Indian in the high Andes falls on my garden in Maine; the same sun shines on us both. If the world's population were to be composed of farmers there would be no wars; it is only when men congregate in cities that they lose their sense of brotherhood.

Mary Russell Mitford, in her everlasting classic *Our Village,* says:

> *Even in books I like a confined locality, and so do the critics when they talk of the unities. Nothing is so tiresome as to be whirled half over Europe at the chariotwheels of a hero, to go to sleep at Vienna, and awaken in Madrid; it produces a real fatigue, a weariness of spirit. On the other hand, nothing is so delightful as to sit down in a country village in one of Miss Austen's delicious novels, quite sure before we leave it to become intimate with every spot and every person it contains; or to ramble with Mr. White over his own parish of Selborne, and form a friendship with the fields and coppices, as well as with the birds, mice, and squirrels, who inhabit them.*

Not a small part of the malaise of this half of the twentieth century is due to our being constantly "whirled half over" the world. Society has become rootless. It is rarely, in these days, that a man lives his life where he was born, and rarer still that he lives in the house of his birth, though there is a deep yearning, especially among the young, for the more stable society of former times. Perhaps some of the happenings of today that we are apt to consider privations will instead prove to be blessings.

Mothers-in-Law

Mothers-in-law have been the butt of humorists' jokes from time immemorial. They have been pictured as destroyers of happy youthful marriages in the same manner that stepmothers have invariably been depicted as mean and cruel to their stepchildren. I suppose there are some who fit that pattern, but my personal experience is to the contrary. Although I never actually had a stepmother, I was raised by an English grandmother who had an uncivilized American five-year-old she had never before seen dropped into her lap and into her Edwardian household, and left there for sixteen years. If that would not bring out stepmotherly attitudes, I don't know what would. I have to report, though, that while she was never mean or cruel, she very quickly taught me to say "Thankyouverymuch" for every favor, to pull out chairs for ladies, to rise to give one my seat, to open doors for them, and to address my male elders as "Sir."

About mothers-in-law I know a little more. I have had two, and neither of them would fit the music hall billing. The first one was pure Victorian, a little Methodist woman who let her husband win all the battles but reserved winning of the wars for herself. She was very proper, and told me that she never called her husband by any name but Mr. Jones. "Not even in private?" What I meant was "in bed," but I didn't dare use the word. She habitually said "limbs" for "legs," but as she had found time, somehow, to have seven children, she must have been less formal in the dark.

She was of that generation of wives who put on their nightgowns first and disrobed under them. I do not say this to disparage her, because she was very kind and non-interfering. Of course I never lived in the same house with her after I married her daughter, which would have been the real test. There is never room for two women in the same house, particularly if they are mother and daughter. Inevitably the day comes when somebody hangs the pot on the wrong hook and there is hell to pay.

My current mother-in-law, who does live with me, although in a separate and adjoining house (I was smart enough for that), is equally unmother-in-lawish. She lives in her own quarters, does her own housecleaning and laundry, cooks her own meals and, periodically, invites us to dine with her. There is nothing very noteworthy about this, you will say, until I tell you that she recently celebrated her ninety-fourth birthday. Helen drops over to chat with her every day and she, in turn, dines with us, but not very often. When she does, she leaves for her apartment as soon as things are cleaned up and she has had a chance to repeat her little formula of "Thank you for my nice dinner."

Like most people of her generation she was born on a farm, but when she was twelve years of age went to the city to live with relatives and soon got a job. Kids went to work early in those days. She did, and kept at it until she was past seventy. She did not and does not have much respect for people who don't work and support themselves. Industry and cleanliness are her twin gods. She maintains you can always get a job if you are content to take what is offered (and she has proved it by never having been out of work during her working years), and that there is no excuse for being dirty. Water is free and soap is cheap.

Mom, for that is the affectionate name everyone uses, lived in or close to a big city all her adult life, and when we thought of bringing her to Brooklin, Maine, which really *is* in the country (no exurbia), we had our doubts about her ability to adjust. We pushed it, though, because nowadays a big city is no place for an elderly lady to live alone. Being afraid to walk to the stores, as she had done for so many years, she agreed reluctantly to come to us. We need have had no fear, for she has taken to the country like a duck to water. She has had a little trouble learning to buy ahead, for she now has to go thirty-five miles to do her shopping instead of riding downstairs in an elevator and walking across the street. Other than that, she has few problems. Being quite deaf, she is compensatingly observant and nothing escapes her sharp eyes. When we take her shopping she notes everything we pass on the way and often sees things we miss.

She has our big yellow tomcat for company. A couple of nights ago, when she went to the door to put him out for his evening excursion, she found another cat looking in through the glass. She said it was the biggest, wildest looking cat she ever saw, and when I told her that from her description it probably was a wildcat, a lynx, that there were some around here, she replied, "Well, whatever it was, I didn't want him looking in my door so I stuck a newspaper across the glass so he couldn't see what I was doing."

Except for one brief visit, Mom had not been to a doctor for twenty-five years, and when we took her to the hospital for a routine checkup the other day, she treated the whole affair as a great adventure. She didn't think it at all necessary but went along just to please me. As on her previous medical encounter, twenty-five years before, there was nothing wrong with her and she told me it was too bad I had made her waste her money. She said to Helen that she didn't like taking off her clothes in front of a man and, when my wife replied that she didn't do any such thing, that the nurse disrobed her and put her under a sheet, she seemed disappointed that her story had been spoiled. I said, "Mom, you must have taken off your clothes in front of a man when you were married," to which she responded, "I sat on the floor on the other side of the bed where he couldn't see me."

When it was all over we took her to our local pizza joint where she drank a bourbon sour and ate a dish of spaghetti and meat sauce, following which she pushed her wagon around the supermarket for half an hour, complained about the price of food and, when we got home, thanked me for a wonderful day.

I guess that in addition to being lucky in love, I am lucky in mothers-in-law, although I still think it would be a bad idea to have one live in the same house with me.

Drilling a Well

I spent most of one afternoon last week watching a huge machine grind inexorably through foot after foot of rock (and my pocketbook) in an effort to find water to supply a cottage we own. Not much water was needed as the place is used only during the summer by our children, grandchildren, and other assorted guests, and is not equipped with such water guzzlers as washing machines and dishwashers. Nevertheless, some water the cottage has to have, and the line that has served it until now, running from the farm, under the road, across the pasture, down around the rocks, and through the woods, has proven vulnerable. Early or late in the year it is apt to freeze, and during the summer cows step on it and the tractor unearths it. Also, it seems that our friends' affection for us extends over a longer period than it did in years gone by when the season was bounded at one end by the Fourth of July and at the other by Labor Day.

I have not had much personal experience with drilling, other than as a miniscule investor in some oil wells, but I learned early from an old casing hand in Texas that you never know what is at the bottom of a hole until you get there. In retrospect I recall that I was fantastically successful in striking water and only on the rarest of occasions in discovering oil or gas. We did not find water in such eyedropper quantities as five or six gallons a minute either, but in hundreds of gallons that the authorities made us pump back into the ground through other holes, some of them our own unsuccessful drillings, and some representing the blasted hopes of other investors. Quite often, too, the water was salt, though the field was hundreds of miles from the ocean.

Water is drilled for, around here, by one of two methods, either the old pounder or the modern rotary drill. Some say the rotary drill closes the small veins in the rock and you get water sooner with the pounder. That has not been my experience and, in any event, I want to know my fate sooner ("If it were done when 'tis done, then 'twere well it were done quickly"), and the rotary does not keep you too long in suspense.

When I saw Mr. Jones's bit grinding down through the granite all my old gambling habits began to reassert themselves. I remembered that when we drilled a well in the village at the library we got twenty-five gallons a minute at about fifty feet, when all we needed was enough water to wash hands and flush the toilet. I reminded my wife that our neighbors a little farther along the shoreline had found plenty of water at about the same depth. Having seen me in this frame of mind before, she merely remarked that both the wells at the farm were over 225 feet deep and did not give us any astonishing supply of water, at that.

The bit ground on, rapidly at first through pink granite, more slowly when it got into gray. The only water coming out of the hole was what was going into it to wash out the chips. Finally at eighty-five feet, the drillers got hungry and knocked off for the day. I did not blame them. Drilling is hard, heavy, wet work. The casings are heavy, the drills are heavy, the drill stems are heavy, all the other things I don't know the names of are heavy, and for a well that does not yet produce water, everything is amazingly wet, including the drillers.

There is one well around here on Naskeag Point that is a real artesian well; it is self-flowing. When it came in, a couple of years ago, before the house it was to supply was built, it was left uncapped over the winter. All winter long, over a mountain of ice, it continued to flow strongly. That, I said to Helen, is what we are going to get. She looked at me pityingly and asked if I would not like to have my pre-dinner drink at the cottage, instead of at the farm, so that I could be there to see it if the well suddenly blew its top like Old Faithful. I replied that I would, and we did, and it was very enjoyable by the shore listening to the whistle of the wings of the sea ducks as they took off in formation to wheel and land with a splash in front of us. But there was no subterranean rumbling from the water hole.

It was ten o'clock before I got to the cottage the next morning. The drill was still turning but the boys were washing up.

"How's it coming?" I asked.

"Five-and-a-half gallons at 145 feet," was the answer. "It's all right. Good water. Taste it. It'll be a bit oily."

It was, but what is a smidgen of lubricating oil to an old oilman?

C'est la Vie

I had heard, while I was away, that there had been a blessed event among our bovine population, so when I got home I hurried to the barn and found our pretty young Guernsey, Cindy Too, in the calving pen with her first offspring. The new arrival was a little bull, all clean and shiny, with a white blaze on his forehead, wobbling about on knobby knees butting his mother's udder.

Helen soon joined me for a look at him and said, "Oh, how cute!" and then added, "but I am not going to see him any more." She will, of course, but it will be in the guise of veal scaloppine. We are careful not to make pets of the animals that are to wind up in the pot. It would probably be less

104

exacerbating to buy our veal in the supermarket but it would not be very good veal, and anyway I think we would be ducking the issue. We often have visitors from the city or suburbs who blench when I point out some animal as being destined for the freezer and say to me, "How can you?" My stock answer is that if they feel so badly about it they should be vegetarians and not be hiring paid assassins to do their killing for them. Country folk rarely make a comment—they are more matter of fact.

I was reminded while in the barn that we were out of hens. Last year we struggled along with eight or ten elderly birds that laid wonderfully large brown eggs in decreasing numbers. We had bought them as pullets a couple of years before, lost half the flock almost at once to some obscure avian distemper, and watched the rest decline into decrepitude and senility until they reached the stage where we wrung their necks and consigned their corpses to the foxes and crows.

When I was a boy I spent part of my morning visit to the barn kicking protesting broodies off the eggs that I had been sent to collect. Once off, they squatted like ducks and shuffled around looking for something to keep warm. They were easy to please—pebbles or china eggs were quite acceptable. The modern hen has no trace of motherhood in her admittedly feeble mind, and you never get a broody unless you can come by an old-fashioned breed like a Buff Orpington, a Minorca, a Rhode Island Red, or a New Hampshire Red, and this is not easily done.

When I was in the Checkerboard paying my feed bill the other day, I heard some peeping in the background and found that it came from a paper bag in the hand of the lady next to me. She had a half-dozen day-old chicks that she said she was going to add to her varied barnyard collection. She admitted to having a lady goose that was laying, and wanted to know where she could find a gander. The proprietor, who is an encyclopedia of information on such matters, provided her with the answer. Further talk led to the admission on her part that she maintained quite a backyard farm in the middle of one of our nearby towns. I won't mention the town, as they have an ordinance against keeping livestock and I have no intention of bringing down the majesty of the law upon a fellow farmer. One of her more pressing problems was that she owned a rooster who, as roosters will, crowed at the day's dawning. She had been to the veterinarian to see what could be done to silence the bird, and showed me some pills that, she had been assured, would take the decibels out of his boasting. What other effect they might have upon him was not revealed. I told her I thought it was a hell of a thing to do to a rooster, and secretly wished I could feed a few to some of the more vociferous prophets of doom who crowd the universities and the airwaves nowadays.

I asked her, "Do you have a broody on your 'farm' or are you going to

put those chicks under a brooder?" She replied, "I'll just keep them in the kitchen," which gave me an idea, so that I, too, left with a box of day-olds. I don't own a brooder either, and indulgent as my wife is, I think she would view with something less than enthusiasm my making a hen-run out of the kitchen. Upon inquiry I learned that a couple of dozen chicks can be accommodated comfortably around the outside of a good-sized pail that has a few inches of sand in the bottom and a 300-watt light bulb hung in the middle. Chicks, having no more brains than their progenitors, huddle cosily around a hard, warm pail and think they are cuddled under the feathery bosom of an old-fashioned hen.

At the moment my chicks, with their pin feathers already sprouting, are domiciled in a cardboard box on top of the potting shed bench, but in a few more days are going to be put into the henhouse. It won't be quite so cosy but I shall be able to lock them in where our dog and cats can't murder them. I know they have designs on the birds, just as I do on the calf.

A friend to whom I was showing my future veal a couple of days ago said, when Cindy Too ducked her horns at me, "That cow knows you are up to no good." How true, how true. *C'est la vie*. We all come to a bad end.

Time Slays All

I plucked the first rose from my garden yesterday and it is beside me on my desk as I write, as fragrant as though this were a hot summer day instead of thick-a-fog, as it is.

I do not have many of the hybrid tea and floribunda roses that are grown and planted by the million all across the breadth of America. It is not that I dislike them, or that I do not think them beautiful, but that where I garden, they live dangerously if they live at all. I have an uncongenial soil for roses, a thin sandy loam over gravel, whereas they revel in heavy clay. The old-fashioned types will put up with sand whereas their more delicate sisters pine and die. Then, too, roses have to brave our climate with winter temperatures normally reaching from ten to fifteen degrees below zero, and a bitter wind off the western ocean that is little subdued by the offshore islands. I did, once, have a magnificent bed of glorious red Frenshams, and cossetted them along with soil mounded over them, and old hay within a burlap shield around them, and for two years they pulled through, but for no reason that I could determine, when the third spring came they did not quicken.

While I can understand those who endeavor to grow plants unsuited to the climate (I did it myself when I was younger), I no longer take pleasure in looking at an invalid. I would rather admire a vigorous crab apple than suffer with a dogwood that is existing on the edge of the outer limits of its zone of hardiness. It is because of this preference that most of my roses are those generally known as shrub, or old-fashioned, roses. I enjoy the old cabbage roses, the moss roses, the albas, Gallicas, rugosas, and the like. True, many bloom but once, though some are remontant, but they are all rock hardy and need no other help than a stake to prevent the winter gales from tearing them out of the ground. My visitors are apt to pass them by because they have been conditioned to think of the more elegant, but more tender hybrid teas as the norm. Perhaps the cabbage rose, the hundred petaled rose, is not as svelte, not so much the sophisticated lady, but she is more faithful and robust, as a blushing country girl should be.

I have many books about roses in my library, books both old and new, among them Dean S. Reynold Hole's *A Book About Roses,* which was first published in 1904. He was the great English rosarian of the nineteenth century. Last night in bed I was reading *In a Gloucestershire Garden* by another wearer of the cloth, Canon Ellacombe, who had 258 species and varieties in his one-and-a-half acre garden. I have innumerable illustrated nineteenth-century books on roses, and the three modern volumes by Graham Stuart Thomas specifically on old-fashioned roses. One that I do not own and probably never shall, as it is both extremely rare and very expensive, is a little book by Nicholas Monardes entitled *De Rosa et partibus eius.* It was published in 1551 and is thought to be the earliest book on the subject. Long after Monardes's death his name was commemorated for us modern gardeners by Linnaeus who gave our common bee balm, or Oswego tea, the botanical name of *Monarda.*

All of these old books, and Mr. Thomas's new ones, are devoted to old-fashioned roses. The hybrid teas are of quite recent origin and were preceded by the hybrid-perpetuals. These latter are less elegant than the hybrid teas, but for the most part quite hardy, and with a few exceptions very fragrant. They are inclined to be once blooming, although an exception is the famous white rose, Frau Karl Druschki, that blooms constantly but is scentless.

Of all species of roses, the one that does best in Maine is *Rosa rugosa.* I suppose it may be called an old-fashioned rose because it was introduced into England as long ago as 1796, but of course long after the real old-timers, like the cabbage rose. It grows so luxuriantly here and survives salt spray, sandy soil, and neglect with such indifference that many people regard it as a wild rose. That it is, of course, but of northern China, Korea, and Japan, not Maine. Like most plants that grow easily, it is not treated with the respect and affection that it deserves. In addition to the type there are now many hybrids. I have half a dozen in my own garden. Besides having magnificent foliage that laughs at all insects and diseases, they are continuous-flowering and delightfully fragrant. Outside the window of my little summer house, where I am writing, is a bush of *Rosa rugosa,* Frau Dagmar Hastrup, five feet high and more across, that is covered with perfectly clear light pink flowers. In spite of the fog that has been with us all morning, the scent of the blossoms is almost overpowering. By and by, when the first flush of bloom has passed, there will be a crop of enormous crimson hips that will intermingle with the next burst of flowers.

Although I would not be without any of the rugosa roses that adorn my garden, there are three others I favor as coequals of Frau Dagmar Hastrup. One of these is *Rosa Parfum de L'Hay,* a cross between a rugosa and a fine old hybrid-perpetual called General Jacqueminot, that even in my poor soil can be treated as a six-foot pillar. It blooms constantly and bears fragrant cherry-red flowers. Another is Sarah Van Fleet, which was introduced by Doctor Van Fleet in 1926. He had a lovely garden in Harrisburg, Pennsylvania. I can still remember wandering around it with him while he wrote notes to his gardener and stuck them in the cleft of a bamboo stake alongside the plant or place that needed attention. It is a good way to remind yourself of jobs to be done, even if you are your own gardener. Sarah Van Fleet has hybrid tea-shaped buds that open to intensely fragrant flat pink flowers. My third favorite is Agnes, which was raised in Canada by T. W. Sanders. Given time, it also will grow six feet tall and four feet across. It has the typical rugosa foliage but it is much smaller than that of its relatives. Its crowning glory lies in the hundreds of small, pompon-shaped yellow flowers with which it is covered. It is considered to be one of the very best of the modern shrub roses, and I do not understand why it is not better known.

Roses, particularly the old-fashioned ones, are not long lasting, but is it not true that the most precious things in life are the most fleeting? That is what makes them precious. Dawn and sunset, the silken skin of a baby, the rose-petal cheeks of the girl you love—time slays all, so enjoy them whilst you may. Remember what Omar Khayyam said:

> *Each Morn a thousand Roses brings, you say:*
> *Yes, but where leaves the Rose of Yesterday?*

The Equation of Time

Among the accomplishments expected of gentlemen in the seventeenth and eighteenth centuries was a knowledge of dialling. The word, in the sense it then conveyed, is unknown today, and I suppose most people now living would associate it with telephoning. What it meant to our ancestors was the ability to design, if not to construct, a sundial. No house or garden of any pretension was without one. It could be as sophisticated as that owned by Charles II, bearing 271 different dial faces, or as simple as the noon mark on a cottage window or the cast pewter dials that are turned out by the Williamsburg Restoration as tourist souvenirs.

The small everyday dials to be found in the gardens and on the houses of those who lived in times when the split second was not important were not very accurate. They had no need to be, but that did not mean that well-made dials could not be, and many were surprisingly so. The secret to sundial accuracy lies in the direction and angle of the gnomon (the vertical element), the level of the dial face, and the table setting forth the corrections for the date. The angle has to be the same as the latitude of the place where the dial is to be erected, and the gnomon must point true, not magnetic, north. The dials one sees offered for sale in garden shops and elsewhere are, almost always, merely decorative as they are not specifically made for the spot where they are to be used.

Clocks, by which we moderns conduct our affairs, mark a constant time, which is an average of the length of the solar days of the year, but the days are not the same and thus the sundial is more accurate, as it indicates local apparent time. As anyone who has been a navigator well knows, the difference between "clock time," which is called mean time, and local apparent time, which the sundial shows, is termed "the equation of time," and is to be found in nautical almanacs. The really good old sundials carried a table engraved upon them that could be applied to get mean time.

Sundials belong to gardens. Accurate or not, their presence creates a feeling of tranquility, a sense of timelessness and "sweet sorrow" that lies at the heart of any true garden. Austin Dobson, who has written with such feeling about times long past, said of sundials:

'Tis an old dial, dark with many a stain;
In summer crowned with drifting orchard bloom,
Tricked in the autumn with the yellow rain,
And white in winter like a marble tomb;
And round about its gray, time-eaten brow
Lean letters speak—a worn and shattered row:
"I am a shade; a Shadowe too arte thou:
I marke the time: saye, Gossip, dost thou soe?"

Our forebears were a good deal more conscious of the uncertainty of life than are we (although death still gets us all in the end, even if we do delay its arrival a bit), and a dial seemed to them to be a good place to remind themselves of this insecurity. I have in my own garden a sundial that does just that. It bears the inscription *Thomas Dryden—London Fecit 1675,* and I like to think that it might have been owned by a relative of John Dryden the poet, who was born in 1631 and died in 1700, and that he composed the lines surrounding it. It is now more than 300 years old and is worn and green with the passage of the seasons. Though time has blurred the letters it is still possible to distinguish:

Amyddst Ye Flowres I Tell Ye Houres
Tyme Wanes Awaye As Flowres Decaye
Beyonde Ye Tombe Freshe Flowres Bloome
Soe Man Shall Ryse Above Ye Skyes

I have always liked Dryden; it was he who said:

Happy the man, and happy he alone,
He who can call today his own;
He who, secure within, can say,
Tomorrow, do thy worst, for I have lived today.

and

For present joys are more to flesh and blood
Than a dull prospect of a distant good.

And men who are unhappy in their wives enjoy the epitaph he intended for his:

Here lies my wife: here let her lie!
Now she's at rest, and so am I.

Almost all sundials are inscribed with mottoes. The modern dials that one picks up in garden shops don't offer much in the way of variety; usually they display the hackneyed old "I Count None But Sunny Hours" that was on old dials too, but was usually in Latin (*Horas Non Numero Nisi Serenas*), a language unintelligible to most people today except classical scholars, who are an endangered species.

It is difficult for people living in an age of time signals and electric watches to realize the place that sundials had in the everyday lives of our ancestors. The first set of paper currency issued by the American Congress included a note, for a third of a dollar, that carried a print of a sundial with the motto "Fugio, Mind Your Own Business." The Franklin cent exhibited a similar design and motto.

Sundials were common in public places even into the early nineteenth century, and most of them carried a moral injunction. "Begone About Your Business" was a favorite. Others were "As A Shadow Such Is Life" or alternatively, "Life's But A Shadow, Man's But Dust, This Dyall Says Dy All We Must."

Sundials were even made with flowers. Linnaeus, the originator of the binomial system of plant names, made a list of forty-six that could be used to tell time. When I was young I used to recite old Andrew Marvell's lines "To His Coy Mistress," but now I am an old gardener I stick to his less dangerous ode to a floral sundial:

> *How well the skillful gardener drew*
> *Of flowers and herbs this dial new.*
> *When from the milder sun*
> *Does through a fragrant zodiac run;*
> *And as it works the industrious bee*
> *Computes its time as well as we!*
> *How could such sweet and wholesome hours*
> *Be reckoned but with herbs and flowers.*

"Hello, Brown Cow"

"Hello, brown cow."

A couple of days ago I was eating lunch beside the kitchen window when, looking out, I saw a hairy young man in careless attire strolling along on the opposite side of the road. The sight was not unusual, for a lot of people pass here to admire the view, although most of them drift by in cars rather than on their own feet. What made this event different was not only that the person was walking (for there are still a few, usually young, who are content to go slowly enough to see something), but that tagging along, fifty feet behind, was a diminutive citizen three or four years old. He held a stick in one hand and was hitching up his pants with the other. Even though his father (I suppose it was his father) was proceeding at a very leisurely pace the boy was having a hard time keeping up. There was the problem of his legs being only a fifth as long as his sire's, but there was also the fact that he was wandering in a world of wonder, the Elysian fields, that caused him to stop, look, and listen, every yard or so. A Scotty named Lord Lancaster, which once owned me as master, was beset by the same troubles. He used to accompany me on walks to Naskeag Harbor, a couple of miles each way, but by the time we got home he had probably traveled ten. Even in his old age the world was a place of incomparable delight, of marvel piled upon miracle.

Gail, who helps out around here, saw my young passerby before I did. She was in the dooryard as he approached and she saw him go up to the fence and address Cindy Too, who was busy chewing her cud and switching off flies. "Hello, brown cow," he greeted her and, if the disparity in length of leg between him and his companion had not cut short his visit, Cindy would have ambled over and licked whatever part of his anatomy was within reach of her long, rough tongue. He could not wait, though. Already the disciplines of life had begun to shackle him.

It is difficult to retain the clear eye and inquiring mind of youth. There are so many enemies waiting to whip you into line. There is, of course, your job, the need that most of us have to make a living. There are the mores of the society in which we live, the need to cut our hair in an acceptable fashion, or to wear a tie, or shine our shoes, or to marry the person we are sleeping with; but do not jeer, my young friends. In your society you are equally disciplined to do the opposite of these things. You must wear disheveled clothing, a ragged beard, long hair, and be contemptuous of the "establishment" and "Victorian morals."

We all, regardless of where we stand in the order of things, become captives of the social group we inhabit. It is the ability to view ourselves objectively, and to accept the fact that we *are* so conditioned, that makes it possible for us to see what is really going on. If we can attain this we can keep the golden age that is the birthright of youth but which, if not guarded, is filched from us by every breath we draw.

My young visitor could not dawdle to enjoy all the new and delightful smells and sights and experiences that assailed him. He was enslaved by long-legs striding off ahead of him, but he was conscious that fairyland lay on every side. He knew "we are such stuff as dreams are made on." There was the goldenrod just coloring into bloom; the thin vapors of fog drifting across the shore pasture; the orange berries of the rowan tree heavily pendulous at the tips of the drooping branches; the brightly colored hollyhocks and phlox and geraniums in my dooryard, and the sight and smell of that huge animal slowly moving its jaws and coming toward him. It was all new and fascinating. Perhaps he had never seen a cow before, except in a coloring book, but he had no fear even though it weighed twenty-five times more than he did. He would have enjoyed examining it more closely as my grandchildren did when they were young, in the days when I took them to the barn on Christmas Eve to see the cattle kneel to the newborn Lord. Cows do kneel, you know. Whenever you go into the tie-up they will rise to greet you, hind end first, so that they are on their knees for a moment.

My neighbor has a long road ahead of him, one beset with dangers that I have never experienced. The old order is broken, and to live with the new one will take more elasticity than I possess. There are dark clouds in his future. Man, today, is no more moral, no less cruel and selfish than he has ever been, and now he has at his command weapons that make the bombs that devastated London and Berlin look like Chinese firecrackers. Somehow, though, he will come through. Man is tough and infinitely adaptable, and though the society he will inhabit will be alien to our experience, he will survive. Not one small boy, perhaps, but mankind will adjust, and having never known the past will make do with what it has, and go on thanking God for man's unconquerable soul.

When I was a young sailor I was told to keep my eyes above the horizon if I wanted to find the light I was seeking. Dag Hammarskjöld said much the same thing:

"Never look down to test the ground before taking your next step; only he who keeps his eye fixed on the horizon will find his right road."

If my young visitor can keep his eyes clear to see the world about him, the dawn and the sunset, the fields and woods and the sea, and can remain sensitive to all the small daily happenings, he will make it.

"Hello, brown cow."

The Spokie Tuft of Thrift

A visitor to my garden, who spends her summers in Scotland and her winters in New Zealand (where it is summer when she gets there) asked me, a few days ago, what was that pretty flower edging a border of roses. I answered that it was thrift. I was surprised she did not recognize it because she is a good gardener, and her summer abode is a country where old things are appreciated. I like thrift and have grown it, off and on, for years. It is an old-fashioned flower, not much seen these days, but still worthy of a place in any dooryard garden, particularly where one wants to create a feeling of intimacy and an association with times long past.

Old John Gerard mentions thrift in *The Herball,* saying:

> *Thrift is a kinde of Gillofloure, which brings forth leaves in great tufts, thicke thrust together, among which rise up small tender stalkes of a spanne high, naked and without leaves; on the tops whereof stand little floures in a spokie tuft, of a white colour tending to purple.*

His description is accurate, even to the "spokie tuft." I cannot define "spokie" but it just fits the appearance of the flower. I must, though, part company with him when he says it is of "a white colour tending to purple." There is a horticultural variety that is white, but from seed it shows a great variability in shades of purple, most light but some almost red. I think the best way to describe thrift to a person unfamiliar with it is in the variability of color and the shape of the leaves and also that it does not smell like onions.

It is an edging plant par excellence; the small tufts of leaves, much shorter than chives, grow uniformly in soldierly precision, surmounted by those "spokie" tufts of flowers that bloom for most of the summer. Alice Morse Earle, in her *Old Time Gardens,* refers to thrift as an edging long in use, and describes it as bordering sundial gardens. For edging, I class it with sweet alyssum, ageratum, and other running ribbons of color, although it has the advantage of being perennial.

Thrift, which is botanically *Armeria,* is allied to statice, or as it is now called, *Limonium.* Sometimes I think it would be better if we who garden for fun just forgot all these nuances and changes; but then, if we did, I suppose we would not be able to order what we want from the seedsmen and nurserymen (although they take off on their own nomenclature occasionally, confusing things still more). Anyway, as I was about to say before I was botanically interrupted, thrift or sea pink, as it is also known, is a seashore plant like the sea lavender that grows wild along parts of our shoreline here in Maine. The difference is that thrift grows wild along the shores of Spain and the Mediterranean. Because of this marine character it shows a preference for sandy soil, which is a good thing for me as that is all I have to offer. It is not averse, however, to being fed and will make a much stronger plant in your garden (although perhaps not as long-lived) than it does growing along the rim of the ocean.

Both thrift and sea lavender grow readily from seeds, as indeed do all of the statice tribe, so if you cannot find plants in your nearby greenhouse, a small packet of seeds will amply care for your needs. Both these plants are evergreen, as are many that inhabit the littoral, and though in this climate they do not look like much in winter, the dull green leaves are there and, if you have covered them with brush, will soon spring to life when the snow goes off.

The flowers of sea pinks being as variable in color as they are, the observant gardener has an excellent opportunity to propagate the plants he considers most desirable and thus build up a superior stock. Among the last couple of dozen I grew from seed is one plant, shorter than the rest, that has deep rose-red flowers. Either in September, or next spring, if I don't lose the marker, I shall dig it and divide it into several pieces and immediately replant them. If I do this for a couple of years I shall have all the plants I want and can discard those I think less desirable.

For people who have no interest in things non-utilitarian, thrift's look-alike, chives, make a good edging plant besides being useful in a culinary way. As the summer wears on chives become untidy, which thrift does not, but they may be trimmed back from time to time to keep them from flopping over on the grass or path, and the clippings can be chopped, placed in a plastic bag, and put in the freezer to be used as a garnish throughout the year.

The Natives

I have been having trouble with the natives lately. Not the ones on two legs who have been around for the last couple of hundred years, but those with four legs who were already in possession when the foreigners from Europe arrived.

It all started in mid-May when a marauding deer broke down a white ash sapling I had transplanted from the woods, and then, a couple of weeks later, nibbled back to hard wood all the new growth on a recently planted double pink crab apple called Plena Nova. My city visitors exclaim over the beauty and grace of the deer in my back pasture and exhibit signs of shock when I say I prefer venison in my refrigerator. But then, they have not had to pay for 600 feet of six-foot-high wire mesh fence to keep deer out of their vegetables.

Things pile up. I was still cussing the deer when my friend Butterscotch came limping across the dooryard toward me one morning, saying as plainly as a cat could, "Look here now. See the mess I'm in. Get busy."

I could have answered "Well, it's your own fault. Who ever heard of a cat taking on a porcupine?" But I didn't, and while my wife held him, I extracted half a dozen quills from the pads of his front feet. At that point he had had enough and struggled free. He sat in a corner and regarded me balefully, refusing further assistance. In due course he did the rest of the job himself but will, I think, confine his hunting in future to smaller game, such as the kangaroo mouse he presented me with the other day. I had never seen a kangaroo mouse before, so he furthered my education. They are well named. Butterscotch's specimen could jump three feet from a standing start.

And then there is the story of Mephitis and my wife's mother. Mom is a great believer in the doctrine of cleanliness being next to godliness, only she thinks of it in reverse order, the Lord taking second place. When she has scrubbed her own establishment to within a paint's thickness of its life, she roams abroad seeking dirt elsewhere like the little lady with the scrubbing brush on the Dutch Cleanser cans. A few days ago she was busying herself in the garage while I was working in the potting shed. Suddenly I heard a scream, and a nervous voice saying, "What's that? Something *moved!*"

Rushing to the rescue I found her pointing to a bag of dog food in the corner. When I shifted it there was Mephitis, a baby skunk, about as large as a fair-sized kitten. As soon as it saw me, it fled into another corner behind some boards. Mom fled into her apartment.

After doing a little staff work I decided to push the wood around a bit, thinking that the skunk would head for the open door. My plan of action was wrong, for suddenly Mephitis switched ends and I found myself looking directly into the muzzle of the gun at a range of about three feet. Either because it was inexperienced in the use of its armament or because it sensed that I had no ill intent, it didn't pull the trigger. I decided not to push my luck.

That night we left the garage door open and in the morning Mephitis was gone, leaving not a trace of fragrance to sully the purity of the Maine coast air.

Early this spring I bought twenty-five day-old chicks and, except for three that departed this life within forty-eight hours of their birth, I carried them through to young ladyhood. Last week they began to lay, which has given me an excuse to eat pullet egg omelet for breakfast, telling myself the eggs are too small to sell and that they are good only for scrambled eggs, or omelet, where they lose their identity.

Yesterday, when Albert Allen gave me his morning paper to read, he said, "We lost three pullets last night," a piece of local news I found considerably more interesting than what was going on in Washington.

"How?" I asked.

"Don't know for sure," he answered. "Something ate their heads off, and a good part of the breasts."

We thought first of skunks, because we knew they were around, but finally exonerated them and laid the murders to a coon, as the hens are inside a six-foot wire fence and coons are a good deal better gymnasts than are skunks.

I don't know where the next assault will come from but we are keeping our guard up and our powder dry and we will wait until we can see the whites of their eyes.

Minor Pleasures of Life

A book that for many years has never been far from my bedside is an anthology, selected and arranged by Rose Macaulay, called *The Minor Pleasures of Life*. I do not lend my copy because it is long out of print, and I have discovered that books, unlike cats, are not equipped with any dependable form of homing device; once away from their familiar shelves they are seldom seen again. If you think you would like a copy you should apply to an antiquarian bookseller. There are a few such still around even though The Old Corner Bookstore in Boston, and Leary's in Philadelphia, havens of blessed memory, are no more.

The Literary History of England refers to Miss Macaulay's "acidulous wit" and "profound pessimism." The only novel of hers that I have read (*Told by an Idiot*) bears out that judgment, but I am sure when she compiled *The Minor Pleasures of Life* she was having fun, and cast aside her acidity, though not her wit. As for pessimism, it is notable only by its absence.

I am unable to say whether my personal enjoyment of the minor pleasures of life (about which I often write) is the cause of my affection for the book or whether reading it introduced me to a whole world of happiness that might otherwise have remained unappreciated. It is sometimes difficult to determine primary causes—the chicken or the egg—but that knowledge is unimportant provided one gains pleasure out of the end result.

I thought of Rose Macaulay yesterday afternoon when, after laboring contentedly and a bit stiffly in my garden all day, I came in and luxuriated in a hot bath. There are, I think, few things better calculated to wash away the frets and annoyances of life than a steaming bath after a day's hard labor. The daily bath when one has not been working and is apparently quite clean is merely a duty, a nod to convention, but the same act when one is sweaty and dirty, and the by-products of one's ablutions whirl in soapy curds down the drain, is another matter. To confer its full blessing the bathwater should be quite hot. In my childhood in the country hot water did not issue from a faucet at the turn of a tap but came out of the spout of a large kettle. It was close to boiling and not much was needed to elevate the temperature of the well water in the galvanized washtub that small boys bathed in. Even today, when I lower myself into the bath, those minor pleasures of childhood return in memory.

The Romans were great bathers, as is evidenced by the first-class facilities they left for posterity to admire. Winston Churchill is said to have observed that not until after 1900 did the bathing apparatus of the British equal that which the Romans had left behind when they departed in the fourth century. In that connection Rose Macaulay reminds one of the report that the Emperor Commodus bathed seven times a day, and that Robert Burton, in his vastly entertaining book, *The Anatomy of Melancholy,* said of the Romans that "rich women bathed themselves in milke, some in the milke of 500 shee asses at once," an activity that one must view rather in the light of conspicuous consumption than any earnest effort at cleanliness.

The English upper classes, practicing a form of self-flagellation, bathe in ice water—at least they did when I was a schoolboy—and the rest of society bathed only during the summer at the seaside. Perhaps because of my early introduction to cold baths I have studiously avoided them the rest of my life. The only thing that cold water is good for is to mix with whiskey— and then only in extreme moderation.

Warm fragrant baths and large fluffy towels should be appropriated to the sole use of small children between the ages of four months and four years. Younger than that they are apt to slip through your hands and drown, and when they are beyond the fourth year they become too angular and boisterous to hold. One of the minor pleasures of life is to watch a two-year-old sailing a duck in a bathtub. There are few more innocent occupations and babes are usually ready to go to sleep afterward, giving their elders a few moments' peace and a chance to use a drop or so of cold water in the manner I previously suggested.

"This Is the Book of Sydney Pickering"

The sheet of paper I had in my typewriter began a column with the words of Montaigne: "It is not death, it is dying that alarms me." But when I told the females of my household what I was intending to write about, they expressed such dismay I decided to postpone the subject to a later date. It is, however, only pushed onto the back burner and may be expected on some other dismal day.

Today is a "drismal" day, a day of rain and fog (the third in a row) that shows no likelihood of changing its mind at least until evening. In addition to making it impossible for me to work in the garden, the cold makes me apprehensive about the welfare of 100 day-old chicks in the barn. True, they have their warm pail half filled with sand, which is heated by a 300-watt light bulb, to comfort them, but the outside temperature was forty-eight degrees at six o'clock this morning and is not much more now.

However, I have done my part and if the Lord in His inscrutable wisdom decides to terminate their lives with pneumonia before they are big enough for me to chop off their heads, I shall, I suppose, like Job, have to submit.

Being deprived of mortality as a subject I turned to my bedside table for inspiration. It was, as usual, piled high with books. When they elevate to the point where I am no longer able to reach the light switch, I return them to their proper shelves and start all over again. Such a periodic house-cleaning came about this morning. In the process I found a small leather-bound volume entitled *Amphora* precariously underpinning several larger volumes—much as the low man in an acrobatic team in the circus holds aloft an impossible number of other members of his troupe. I had forgotten it was there and wondered why it was, until I discovered between its pages a plastic wrapper (from a Di-Gel tablet) I had used as a bookmark. What it marked was a poem that had been inspired·by a handwritten dedication in an old edition of Cowley's poems. The poem is a little too long to quote in full so you will have to hunt it up yourself, but I will give you the first stanza, which is utterly charming. It goes:

> This *is the book of Sydney Pickering,*
> *My sometime Lover and my always King,*
> *Whom I do* utterly *love and adore,*
> *Now as before.*

I do not know why this arrangement of words is so appealing to me but it is. Miracles like this have happened before and will, I am sure, happen again. I think the first time such a happiness came over me was when I read gentle, fey Ophelia's ". . . There's a daisy; I would give you some violets, but they withered all when my father died." Shakespeare has this ability to baste together a few words without any apparent effort and to create unforget-table music. Most serious writers manage it at long intervals but Shake-speare seemed not to have even to try. His thoughts just arranged themselves that way. A. E. Housman had a little of the gift too, but I think he had to work harder—though if one works too hard it never happens. He succeeded in *A Shropshire Lad:*

> *Loveliest of trees, the cherry now*
> *Is hung with bloom along the bough.*
> *Now, of my threescore years and ten,*
> *Twenty will not come again,*
> *And take from seventy springs a score,*
> *It only leaves me fifty more.*

But I digress; I started talking about books, not what is in them. *Amphora* is a Maine book. Not that its contents were written by Maine authors but the book was published by the Mosher Press in Portland, Maine, and its contents were selected by Thomas Bird Mosher. Those who are book lovers or booksellers (which is to say the same thing, for I have never met a bookseller who did not love books) will be familiar with the Mosher Press. Many beautifully bound volumes have issued from its doors. Their contents may not appeal to everyone, though they do to me, but no one could fail to admire the books. They are for the most part small in size and fit the hand well. I have over many years accumulated about forty titles and when-ever I see one I set about buying it.

Amphora is bound in three-quarter, slightly faded, green morocco and would be additionally described in a bookseller's catalogue as T.E.G. which, translated for the benefit of those unfamiliar with catalogue English, means top edge gilt. I unashamedly confess a preference for beautifully bound books and I hate with a hatred indescribable those who abuse them:

those miserable sadists who, taking a new book in their hands, bend it back and break the spine from top to bottom; those dreadful wantons who place wet coffee cups on books; those infidels who turn down the corners of the pages; those callous clodhoppers who open an uncut book with their fingers; those thrice-damned excommunicants who leave their greasy paw marks as evidence of their stupidity so all future generations may curse them. I do not mind a few pencil notes on the margins indicating the reader was thinking while reading (I am guilty of this myself) and I delight in signatures, or inscriptions, or bookmarks on end papers that give me a clue to the previous owners.

To a vast number of people a book is merely a thing, like a piece of machinery, or a lawn mower, or an automobile. When it has served its purpose they heave it out with the trash. This, I guess, is fair enough for the sort of books they read. They are the ones who keep drugstore pornographic paperback racks in business. In these days, when half the college population can't read, those who can lavish their bookish affections upon what they can afford—mainly paperbacks—but long for the day when they can see their shelves stacked with authors properly dressed.

I was fortunate enough to have been born when a well-bound book could be bought for a few dollars and when $10 would buy three-quarter leather. I have a White's *Selborne* beautifully bound in red morocco that I paid $10 for, and on my desk beside me is a copy of Repton's *The Art of Landscape Gardening* half bound in hand tooled green levant that still has the price of $15 on the inside back corner. Gardeners will drool over Repton, and bibliophiles over a book designed by Bruce Rogers.

The binding of a book has more to offer than beauty. I, and many others who think as I do, enjoy owning first or early editions of books because the contemporary binding adds a certain flavor to the book itself. A first edition of Dickens's *A Christmas Carol* takes one back with instant magic to the Christmas when it first appeared. Needless to say, I do not own a "first" of *A Christmas Carol* but there are facsimiles that are delightful. Many famous books by American authors—Emerson, Thoreau, Hawthorne, to name but three—could have been obtained until quite recently in their early editions (and some may still be) at very modest prices. The essence of the New England of the time when they were published remains with them and enhances their contents. Some books even smell like their place of origin. I have a two-volume set of Cowper's poems that I bought in Olney. I do not recall what it cost. Not much, I am sure. I also bought another little book from the guardian of Cowper's house (the last one of a small edition about the place). It smells like the watermeadows of Olney and so do the volumes of Cowper's poems that have rested beside it for many years.

If you like bedside books, keep your eye open in the antiquarian book-shops for a copy of *Amphora*. Mosher first published it in 1912, but there were several later editions. Mine is dated MDCCCCXXII. Don't forget to look for:

> This *is the book of Sydney Pickering,*
> *My sometime Lover and my always King.* . . .

Almost My Private Highway

I wandered along the old county road this morning, a road that has led to nowhere ever since the tarred road was made a score of years ago. I say it leads to nowhere, but of course that is not so, for all roads lead one some-where even if, when you get there, it is not where you wanted to go. Robert Frost said:

> *Two roads diverged in a wood, and I—*
> *I took the one less traveled by,*
> *And that has made all the difference.*

This road is not much traveled by either, and after half a mile or so runs into parched grass on the back side of a summer body's barn. It is almost my private highway, for except during July and August when it is used to reach a couple of summer cottages, and again in November when hunters use it, there are no wayfarers to disturb its solitude.

There are some stretches where the firs and spruces reach their arms overhead to make a green aisle; but elsewhere the ledge shoulders through the thin soil and the sun strikes down so strongly that only stunted blue-berries and wild roses struggle to maintain a scanty foothold between the lichen-covered outcrops. At one point a narrower road, barely a car's width, not much more than a path, pitches steeply and erratically toward the shore. It is easy going downhill but calls for a few minutes' rest against a boulder on the way back. Today, as I waited to get my breath, the fragrance of the firs was almost overpowering. The air was still, as it often is on these fall days, and the hot sunshine beating down on the enclosing balsams distilled their aromatic sweetness into a heady fragrance.

Autumn is the time of the year when all growth and development matures into fulfillment. The French call wine the sunshine of France. In a sense, autumn, like wine, is the end product of the sun and the wind and the rain and the fog and the dew and the drought of all the days of the year that precede it.

Autumn in your garden, or in your life for that matter, is a time for contemplation. If you are not happy with what you see, there is not much you can do about it, but there are few gardens so poor, or lives so barren, that a little color and fragrance is not to be found somewhere, distilled from time past, *temps perdu.*

In the Cathedral at Winchester in England, where one's footsteps echo from the stones underfoot into the long vaulted nave, which is exceeded in length only by St. Peter's at Rome, is a memorial window to Izaak Walton. He passed to his reward in 1683 having lived more than ninety years. He was a writer and a fisherman, a gentle man who died beloved of all who knew him. I mention him now because it was written of him that there was a fragrance about his memory, without equal in history, that has endeared him to all succeeding generations. In the window above his grave, in Prior Silkstedes Chapel, is one of his favorite texts, one that he used in *The Compleat Angler*: "Study to be quiet."

There always seems to be in late September a lull in the ongoing of nature, a time of quiet, between summer and the flaming downfall of the year in October. There is a fragrance of memory about autumn that distinguishes it from the other seasons. It is like that interregnum that the Good Book describes for those of us beyond threescore years and ten, a period when we really should not be here at all (for the Bible says that "The days of our years are threescore years and ten; and if by reason of strength they be fourscore years, yet is their strength labor and sorrow; for it is soon cut off, and we fly away") but when the next world is, apparently, not yet ready to receive us. These are the golden days when we walk with nature and our friends and our gardens, and enjoy what hath been wrought. Most of our lives are spent in striving to improve, or anyway to change, but at this moment of calm we are beyond change, so that all we can do is to enjoy what we have.

Stumbling Around the Woods

Along around coon moon time, which is November, newspapers begin to receive letters from indignant citizens weeping over the cruel sport of hunting raccoons. They are as predictable as the appearance of the coon hunters. I have not observed them to be very effective and neither, for that matter, is most coon hunting except for the pleasure that the hunters get out of stumbling around the woods in the middle of the night.

A coon is a pretty smart fellow and not all that easy to do in even if you possess a good coon dog. However, *I* do not hunt coons. Actually I don't hunt anything, except what are known around here as "patridges," and I seldom hit them because I can't see as well as I once did. When my old dog Quince was alive he tried to help me, but now that he is hanging around St. Peter's gate waiting for me to check in, I don't even have a hunting companion. I make this disclaimer because I hope it will prove some defense against those who might write, saying they are disappointed I would act as defense counsel for coon hunters.

When I thought about using coon hunting as a subject I remembered that E. B. White wrote a piece years ago in which he described his participation in a coon hunt. It is a very good story and it all came back to me after I reread a couple of paragraphs. I read no more than that because I knew if I did I would, sooner or later, repeat something he had written; and while I know he would not accuse me of plagiarism, I did not want even to suspect myself. Perhaps it is because my interests and his are similar, or perhaps it is just the magic of his prose, but I find things he said embedded in the matrix of my mind. They are back there along with quotations from Shakespeare, and the King James version of the Bible, *Baron Münchausen, Alice in Wonderland,* and *archy and mehitabel,* and there is no telling when they will float to the surface. Anyway, if you really want to get some measure of the excitement and fragrance of a coon hunt you should read a piece by that name in *One Man's Meat* by E. B. White.

I take no pleasure in killing anything but I am able to do so without lacerating my spirit too much if I intend to use what I shoot for food or some other useful purpose. I would not mind a bit killing raccoons if I could catch them. Last year they cleaned out my whole corn crop in spite of fences, lights, and electric wires, and I think it would have been but reasonable restitution if I had been able to kill one and eat him (or her).

I have eaten raccoon only once in my life and that was so long ago that I have forgotten what it tasted like. However, I had it on the authority of a Negro who used to work for me that it is excellent eating. I mention his race only because those Negroes who live in the country know a lot more about coons than do white men—and a lot more about a good many other country matters, too. He told me also that groundhogs were good fare but, although there were plenty around my place at that time, I was never able to sample one. A groundhog can disappear down a hole faster than you can squeeze a trigger. However, if the opportunity ever presents itself I intend to have either or both on my menu.

I thought I might get a coon this summer but was disappointed. I bought a Hav-A-Heart trap and baited it with some good Maine sardines (which ripened as time passed) but my whole bag was three skunks and our cat. I wondered where the coons had gone until I learned that a neighbor had caught sixteen. I guess he cleaned out the local population.

I have never shot anything in my life just for the thrill but, having a moderately logical mind, I have trouble justifying the attitudes of people who get emotional about the destruction of members of one species of animal life while ignoring others. I would like to make a bet that those who write to newspapers protesting the hunting of raccoons would stamp on a cockroach in their kitchens, or trap any mice they saw there (or certainly any rats) and think nothing of it. Now a rat is a very intelligent animal and can be tamed as easily as a coon, although from a human's point of view their faces are not so appealing. And what about snakes? I happen to like snakes but almost everyone I know hates them, and is unreasonably fearful of them, and will kill them on sight.

I read a piece in a newspaper that described a hunter as climbing a tree in the middle of the night with a gun in his hands in order to shoot a raccoon, but either the facts were slightly cockeyed or the hunter did not have all his buttons. The reason one carries a gun when hunting is to be able to reach the quarry, and I have never seen a tree so tall (not around New England, anyway) that a rifle shot would not reach the top. The accepted procedure in coon hunting is for someone to carry a powerful flashlight and aim it at the coon while the gunner pulls the trigger.

Yes, I know that raccoons are attractive animals if you don't get close enough to them to permit them to bite you, but so are calves and lambs and they don't bite. And a dead racoon is certainly not any deader than a dead lamb or calf, so to be logical, people who don't want coons to be shot should be vegetarians.

Coq au Vin

I devoted most of yesterday afternoon to concocting a *coq au vin,* which is nothing but one of several versions of French chicken stew. Like chicken stews from other countries, you can include in it almost anything you fancy, or on which you can lay your hands. The only compulsory items are the chicken and as much wine as you can afford. I doubt I have ever made two chicken stews exactly alike. The ingredients, other than the chicken, differ with the season and with what happens to be in the larder. The recipe I maltreated yesterday was one given by Roy Andries deGroot in his marvelous cookbook *Feasts For All Seasons.* It calls for up to two bottles of Beaujolais from the town of Fleurie but, as I was out of Beaujolais from Fleurie for the moment, I substituted an Italian wine, a Ruffino del Magnifico. It took a bottle and a half to cover the chicken and we drank the rest. It was a bit heavy but, bearing in mind the amount of garlic and onions and thyme and salt pork I used, it did no great harm. It was, however, not a dish for those who like their food pale, bland, and insipid.

We own two of Mr. deGroot's cookbooks, the one mentioned above and another called *Recipes from the Auberge of the Flowering Hearth.* If you enjoy reading, or if you like to cook, or even better if you indulge in both of these pleasant pastimes and don't own these volumes, go right out and buy them (steal if need be). Mr. deGroot is my favorite cookbook author. Even if you can't boil water the books are worth reading for pure pleasure, though you really do need to be some sort of a cook to use the recipes, as they are a little complicated even if presented in a simple manner. However, I don't think the author intended them for blushing brides whose idea of a gourmet dinner is a box from Colonel Sanders.

Roy Andries deGroot was born in London in 1912, went to St. Paul's and Oxford, worked as a journalist, and suffered injuries during the London blitz that subsequently resulted in blindness. He has lived in this country for many years, is an American citizen, and it is obvious that his handicap has not interfered with his appreciation of good food or his ability to write about it. The only thing I have against him is that he lives in New York but as he can't see it, I suppose that makes it bearable. I hate New York. Even if I couldn't see it I would still hate it because I couldn't avoid smelling it. The only place the gasoline fumes are more compelling in their stench is Los Angeles. God pity the angels.

I am not going to give you deGroot's recipe for *coq au vin* except to suggest in a general way that you should substitute the best part of two bottles of Beaujolais for the water you would ordinarily use in a chicken stew. The reason I won't tell you is not that I am afraid the author would sue me (I don't think he would sue another journalistic cook anyway), but because I want to toll you into buying his books. I have heard it said that blindness sharpens the other senses, which perhaps accounts for his being more than usually specific about the herbs and spices in his recipes. Flavorings are very important in cooking, and so many people never get past pepper and salt. DeGroot has a recipe for mussels that I like particularly (perhaps because I can get the finest mussels in the world by walking out on Naskeag Point and picking them off the rocks), that calls for crystal salt, freshly ground black pepper, parsley, shallots, and, of course, wine. He also calls for plenty of heavy cream, which leads me to believe that either he is not bothered by cholesterol or, like me, has lots of it and doesn't give a damn.

Living where I do, on the edge of civilization according to those who hold city/suburban passports, we get most of our food, except staples, locally. We raise a lot ourselves, too. If I want scallops for dinner (they are also good for breakfast) I ring my friend Louise, whose husband is scalloping this time of year, and she hails him on the CB and he stops at my kitchen door and dips out a quart, or whatever, on his way home from the harbor. Needless to say this way of life calls for eating things when they are in season or, anyway, out of your own freezer. It is because we had a sudden glut of chickens that I made *coq au vin*.

Albert came in a few days ago and said "There must be a hen out. I found an egg under a lilac bush." We caught the hen and returned her to captivity, but I was reminded I was spending more for grain on that particular flock than we were getting out of the eggs. Accordingly, the grim reaper came along and reaped off a couple of dozen heads and now the freezer is full of old hens. I guess you can make *coq au vin* out of store-bought fowl but they won't have much flavor and they will be the wrong color. Admittedly my old layers are tougher than factory raised chickens, but their skins are a nice light yellow whereas the ones from the supermarket look as though they had been raised in a cave among the mushrooms. Suppose they are a little tough. A few hours simmering in a mixture of Gallo's Hearty Burgundy, a slug of rum, garlic, onions, and whatever other spices you fancy, would tenderize the bottom half of a rubber boot, let alone an old hen. And, oh, the flavor!

129

The Annual Countdown

As Christmas once more approaches I am reminded of Carl Sandburg's lines:

> *If I should pass the tomb of Jonah*
> *I would stop there and sit for a while;*
> *Because I was swallowed one time deep in the dark*
> *And came out alive after all.*

Up to this point in time I have always made it through Christmas no matter how dark the prospects may have appeared, but I am, nonetheless, terrified as the annual countdown approaches.

It is not that I am a miserly man, that I do not want to spend my money to make glad the hearts of my fellows here on earth, but rather that the prospect of having to search for something suitable—and not, in my panic, winding up with something utterly useless—paralyzes me.

Christopher Morley once wrote a semiautobiographical book entitled *John Mistletoe* in which he said:

> *If there is any appalling and spiritually murderous sensation on*
> *earth, it is the knowledge that on a certain date or at a given time*
> *and place you have got to be somewhere doing some set, prescribed,*
> *definite thing. This winter we shall keep our horizon perfectly,*
> *crystallinely open, ready every day for the scouring gales of impulse.*

As a sometime mariner I enjoy stormy weather, and am ever ready to spread my sails to "the scouring gales of impulse," but all that impulse will do for you at Christmas is to get you into trouble. You are supposed to perform in a certain predictable manner and if you were, for instance, to send a lady a half-dozen salt haddock that she could eat, instead of a half-dozen handkerchiefs to add to the 100 she already has, you would find people eyeing you with some apprehension.

For some years I postponed my Christmas shopping until Christmas Eve, in the hope that there would be fewer things to choose from and that the stores would be less crowded. Both of these assumptions proved to be correct but it really did not help very much. I still had no more idea of which out of a dozen things I should buy than I had when I used to have to make my selection out of 100.

I am further handicapped by the fact that I am a man and have a feeling that if I go into a store I should buy something. I have noticed that women feel no embarrassment whatever about entering six stores, having a clerk haul out several articles in each one, and ending by not buying anything in any of them.

Probably the worst mistake one can make in selecting gifts is to assume that the recipient will like something because you do. More businesses have ended in bankruptcy by following that theory than any other. I am reminded of it every time I turn on television. If the networks were to offer the programs I like, few other people would look at them. I am sure of it because I rarely see anything I really enjoy and, since NBC and CBS are making money, they must have interpreted the signals correctly from the great mass of the viewing public.

What I prefer to do is to follow John Mistletoe's counsel and make my gifts when impulse, aided by events, suggests the gift and the moment. No one can criticize the practice of Christmas giving, for, as Frank Swinnerton once remarked, "It is very nearly the only remaining sign that we dwellers in the modern nightmare love one another." It seems to me, though, that our compassion and solicitude for our fellows would be better if it were more sustained and not artificially crowded into one day in the middle of winter.

As for myself, I have solved the problem reasonably well by convincing my wife that she is much better qualified to select Christmas presents than I. That leaves me with only one gift to buy—hers, and although at this moment I have not the remotest notion of what it might be, when I finally come to a decision and make the purchase, I depend on her to convince me (as she manages to do every year) that it is exactly what she wanted.

All times
are his seasons

JOHN DONNE

Good Manners

While our avian lunch counter has been open for business for several weeks, no customers showed up until a couple of inches of snow fell a few days ago. The earliest and most raucous arrivals were, as usual, the blue jays. They are beautiful birds but, like some of the "beautiful people" my granddaughter goes into ecstasies over, have very bad manners. Not only do they stand with their feet in the middle of the food, and scream and assault smaller birds, but they stuff their crops—if that is what they have under their chins—until they resemble pouter pigeons. I suppose they come by their bad manners genetically because they are members of the *Corvidae* family, which includes such rowdies as the crows, the ravens, the magpies, and jackdaws.

Watching them this morning it was difficult not to draw a comparison between them and another family of warm-blooded animals, *Homo sapiens*. One can say this, though, for the blue jays: they appear to have leveled off at a plane of impoliteness; while humans, on the other hand, having at one time established a belief that courtesy was a desirable quality, are now retrogressing.

I was interested recently to observe in an airplane lavatory a sign requesting the user to wipe off the washbowl when he was done. In the less enlightened days of my youth such a sign would have been superfluous, for in all the hundreds of Pullman washrooms I have patronized I cannot recall ever seeing anyone neglecting to fulfill this elementary act of consideration for his fellow travelers. It was *de rigueur,* as was refraining from smoking in a lady's presence until permission had been received. Gentlemen got to their feet when ladies entered a room, offered them their seats in a public vehicle, and walked on the outside of the sidewalk so that, if necessary, they could step into the street. One held doors for elderly or handicapped persons, allowed one's female companion to enter a car first, and closed the door behind her before getting in one's self. These, and 100 other acts of politeness, were performed as a matter of custom by all ranks and ages of society. While they may appear to the young, who do not know any better, and to many of their elders, who have become negligent, as hilariously funny survivals of the age of chivalry, they are in fact the lubricant that makes it possible for people, who have no great affection for each other anyway, to get along.

A young lady visitor from a family of good background asked my wife, in some wonder, if we always used the dining room and dressed for dinner. In my youth "dressing for dinner" meant wearing a dinner jacket and a black tie, but that was many years ago and customs have changed. What surprised our young visitor was that we changed from the clothes we had been working in all day and made a small ceremony of our evening meal. We do so because we believe it is important, that there is a certain value in formality. Almost anyone is apt to act in a more civilized manner if he dresses for the part. We are, after all, not too far removed from the savage, as the enthusiasm with which we murder each other, legally, as in warfare, and outside the law, as in shooting errant wives and their paramours, indicates.

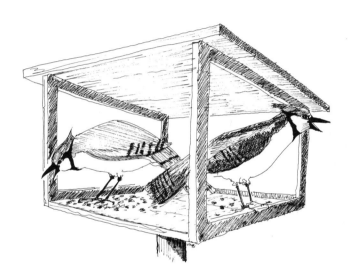

I have a feeling that a not inconsiderable part of the current wave of lawlessness can be blamed on the contempt for good manners that is so prevalent among a large segment of the populace today. It may seem simplistic to suggest that neglecting to push in a lady's chair at a dinner table or taking an axe to one's mother-in-law is part of the same cloth, but it all stems from a lack of consideration for others.

I must confess that I weary of the increasing fractionalization of society. Everywhere we see people splintering into ever-smaller groups, each selfishly laboring to further its special interest. We hear protests from the young that they must be allowed to "do their thing," that they must assert their independence. Bernard Shaw once remarked, "Independence? That's middle-class blasphemy. We are all dependent on one another, every soul of us on earth." He also said that the test of a man's or a woman's breeding was how they behaved in a quarrel (which is something worth remembering).

A generation or so ago we were taught by our elders, as a matter of course, to be mannerly. We said "sir" to those older than ourselves, not to be subservient but because it was realized by everyone that, for society to function smoothly, authority must rest somewhere, and for the young that somewhere was in their elders. As a matter of fact, I still address my elders as sir, although sad to relate, there are no longer many of them.

I don't quite know where we got off the track, because for hundreds of years men had no doubt about the virtue of good manners. It seems to have taken what we are pleased to think of as the most enlightened period of our civilization for us to cast aside what generations of our forefathers laboriously established as a shield against our brutish natures.

We do not need to overthrow society in order to improve man's lot. More can be accomplished by good manners, which are built on consideration for others, than by all the judgments handed down by all the courts of the land. What we need to do is to keep the axle greased, not break up the wagon.

Neighborliness

Few sights are more poignantly expressive of the loneliness of winter than that of a solitary crow laboring heavily into a bitter wind over a frozen rutted field. Winter is a whole season of cold and snow and ice, but its presence is really compelled upon us by small individual occurrences. The calendar may report winter has arrived but it is not winter for us until certain, often quite unimportant, things come to pass.

The essential ingredient of neighborliness is propinquity. One may be possessed of many acquaintances (scattered over half the earth) and a few old friends, but one's neighbors are those with whom one's daily life is enmeshed. In a city or a suburb other lives press in on every side, but there is no neighborliness as we in the country know it, for there is no real propinquity. In a city one may live for years in an apartment house and not even know other people living on the same floor, and certainly not have any involvement in their affairs. In the suburbs community of interest is usually limited to people living on the same street, and even then the individuals are so encapsulated that they revolve in their own fixed orbits like tiny stars in a tiny galaxy.

A friend from one of the faceless suburbs that are creeping like a mold across the country was visiting me last summer. I took him for a ride through the town and along the Reach Road, where off to the left the sun sparkled on the blue water. As we moved slowly along, for we were not really going anywhere, I pointed out the places of interest and told him casually who lived in the several houses we passed and what they did for a living. When we got back home he remarked to his wife that, would she believe it, I knew the name of everybody for ten miles around. This was not strictly true, for there are some, quite a few, I do not know, but that it should be considered remarkable that I know as many as I do, did not occur to me, since most of my neighbors (who have lived here longer) have a wider acquaintance than I.

I do not suggest that because most in our town know one another everything is sweetness and light. After all, we are made up of generous and selfish, kind and unpleasant, young and old, sick and healthy, ordinary people such as compose the human race. There does exist, however, one quality that acts as a leaven on the whole, and that is a sense of belonging, of being a part of an old and stable community, a feeling of love of place that overrides the normal bickerings that even saints (and we are no saints) must become involved in.

This heartwarming climate of neighborliness is never more apparent than when the first stern symbols of approaching winter are to be seen.

Our summer friends are gone and their houses are boarded and shuttered. The early snows drift unplowed in their driveways. The cars on the road are few, and you recognize most of them. It is as it used to be in the old farmhouses where, as the cold set in, the outlying rooms were established in a state of suspended animation for the winter. The parlor was the first to go because it was rarely used anyway; then perhaps the ell bedrooms, and so on until the place shrank slowly in toward the heart, which was the murmuring kitchen stove.

Our town closes in upon itself in the same manner. Its heart is the general store, the post office, the library, the church, and the two schools. If you happen to be at the store at the right time, you will see a jumping, skipping, sliding, multi-colored snake of children pass on their way to or from the "hot lunch." I do not know them all by name, for the generations move along too rapidly as one grows older, but I can distinguish the Smiths, the Allens, and the Tapleys, and some of the other old native families by their characteristic features. The children know me, though, because they have seen me around all their lives and because my wife was on the School Committee. They call and wave, but then they have the advantage, for I am but one, and they are many.

When the first hard storm blows in and the dry snow, carried on a howling easterly gale, sweeps endlessly past my lighted window, the telephone will ring and a voice will say: "Quite a blow, ain't it? You all right? I saw the plow headed down your way. Just thought I'd call and see if your phone was workin'. Ayah, ayah. We're O.K. 'Bye now."

The Snowy Owl

Blue Hill Bay, which has been frozen from shore to shore for several weeks, broke up in yesterday's heavy rain and southerly wind. What had been a vast white field marked only by spruce-covered islands has changed overnight into blue water sparkling in the sunshine under a bluer sky. Fields of ice, some no larger than a bedsheet, others a quarter of a mile across, ebb and flow with the tide. Scallopers, trailed by clouds of gulls, are again dragging slowly back and forth in the foreground.

When I listened to the astronauts describing the cloudless blackness of the sky, and the gray desolation of the moonscape with its bitter clarity unsoftened by an atmosphere, I was reminded—as I have often been before—how much color means in our lives.

When the bay is not frozen, as it rarely is, I am unaware of how much life it contributes to the scene. I think of it as an expanse that is darker than the sky but lighter than the surrounding spruces. I say "I think," but I do not really think about it at all. I accept it. Now, after several weeks of unrelieved absence of color, the water appears startling in its strength. Yesterday I could not have told you how far offshore the white lighthouse stood on its snow covered patch of rock and sand, but today my eyes have regained their depth of vision.

Last week my wife called my attention to a bird flying across our snow covered field. She asked, "Is that a gull?" The bird was flying a few feet above the snow, with long steady beats, and was scarcely visible against the white background. Suddenly it set its wings and coasted upward into a naked hackmatack where it settled on one of the larger branches. It was a snowy owl, but until it got something dark behind it, was quite impossible to identify.

Edward Forbush says that in only one instance has he known an Arctic owl to roost in a tree, so that this bird's perch was unusual. My own experience has been limited, but those I have seen previously have alighted on large boulders. They seem, however, to have a common characteristic of staying in one place for a long time. I first saw this bird before breakfast and it was still motionless at two in the afternoon.

It had not been in the hackmatack very long before a handful of crows arrived to pester it. Crows must learn of the presence of an owl through some form of extrasensory perception, for though there be not a crow in the sky, let an owl alight in a tree and in fifteen minutes it will be surrounded by tormentors. These were braver than I would have been, for there is something sinister about the frozen stance of an Arctic owl. I think the crows sensed it too, for they soon gave up and flew away.

There are those of my friends, who visit in the summer, who ask if it is not lonely here during the winter, many miles from a city and out of sight of any other house. The answer is no, because the hours of the day are never long enough to contain the succession of small happenings occurring around me. Rachel Carson once said that were it possible, her "gift to each child in the world [would] be a sense of wonder so indestructible that it would last throughout life, as an unfailing antidote against the boredom and disenchantments of later years, the sterile preoccupation with things that are artificial, the alienation from the sources of our strength."

Living can be an ever-changing miracle, but it takes cultivation.

140

Prospecting After Spring

I walked down the woods road toward the shore yesterday for the purpose of discovering what signs of spring were in evidence. I was tolled along by the warmth of the sun and the knowledge that my calendar recorded the date as the twenty-first day of March.

I had hoped I might find the tips of a few skunk cabbages emerging from the cold swampy ground where early in the year an apology for a stream makes its way down to the bay. The stream was there all right, quite a respectable trickle that had washed out a corner of the parking area next to the camp, but *Symplocarpus foetidus,* like the groundhog, was still in hibernation.

If you keep your distance the skunk cabbage is an attractive plant. Later in the year when its large green leaves are spread wide, it looks rather like a variety of *Hosta,* or plantain lily, but it is when the purple spathes first emerge from the ground that they are most interesting. One reason they appear so early is that they grow in swampy land where there is enough subsurface water moving to keep the ground from freezing deeply.

There is an exotic skunk cabbage, *Lysichitum americanum,* that I should very much like to grow, as the spathe is butter yellow, but I have never found an American source of supply even though the plant is native to the Pacific Northwest. The seeds I got from England failed to germinate.

In the years we have a robin in winter residence it can usually be found hanging about in the same area. There it is sheltered from the cold northwest wind by the rising ground and protected from the northeasters by the alders that have the same preference for wet feet the skunk cabbage possesses. Woodcock are also fond of alder thickets, as anyone who has carried a gun after them can testify, but I found no woodcock either. Had my old companion, Quince, still been living I might have done better, for the birds lie close and unless you have a dog you may walk through a covey and not know they are there. They would have been a sign of spring too, for occasionally they are seen in early March, and Forbush reports them in Massachusetts in February.

I observed that one alder, out of hundreds that I passed, was in tassel. Why just one I don't know; perhaps the ground was less frozen at that spot or perhaps the alder just naturally came into flower earlier. Most plants exhibit a range in their time of fruition, which is why, for instance, we have early and late apples. The husbandman propagates the extremes to prolong the season.

All the ice was gone along the foreshore, although there were still hard mounds of it on the north side of the enormous boulders that the last ice age left scattered in our woods and fields. In the woods I have seen ice enough to cool a bottle of wine as late as mid-May, but there will not be any this year because we, along with most of New England, have enjoyed a mild winter.

As I wandered along the beach I avoided the wet spots caused by the little brooks and streams that in early spring drain down off the land to soak into the sand and shingle. They look only a little darker in color than the rest of the shore, but if you step into them you will sink in over your ankles. To keep clear I stayed close to the water where the footing was firm and soon wished I had brought a clam hoe with me, for little spurts of water betrayed their presence. I did give thought to going back for one but it was half a mile to the barn and most of it uphill, so I decided to postpone my clam digging until another day. Clams are about all you can dig around here in winter; you can, that is, if you don't mind picking over a few bushels of icy mud. The clams are worth it, though, when you get them. Winter clams taste sweetest.

Mr. H. Johnson must sell more clams than anyone, but they are not like ours. They have no bellies. I once thought he extruded the "clams" like spaghetti but I have learned since that they resemble what we call hen clams, those big old baysters that are ground up to flavor a stew. His come from off the New Jersey coast where they "rush them to dockside processing plants, shuck and thoroughly clean them [there go the bellies], slice them into narrow strips, and freeze." Perhaps if you never ate a real Maine clam these are better than nothing, but you wouldn't catch me digging winter clams if that was to be my reward.

The only other prospector after spring I encountered on my journey was a chipmunk but he did not stop to reveal what he had found. He came out from under a rock on one side of the road and fled across the tar with his tail erect and vanished, without even a nod of recognition, into a stone wall on the other side. Me? I went home and opened a can of clam chowder.

The Grouse that
Flew Through the Window

The evening weather forecast had predicted cloudy skies and occasional light showers, but when I awoke in the night the shutters were rattling and I could hear the steady drumming of rain on the roof. In the morning, as a gray light reluctantly outlined my bedroom windows, it was obvious that the "light showers" had become a heavy and enveloping wind-driven rain.

Sited as we are, ninety-eight feet above the bay and completely open to easterly gales, we take our storms unprotected, like a ship at sea. All day long the house trembled, and the wind rumbled so loudly and continuously in the chimney of my study that when my wife came to ask a question, we had to retreat to the comparative quiet of the living room to carry on our conversation.

Happy, our little Brittany, kept close all day. Most dogs are fearful of thunder, and she, I am sure, mistook the growling and thumping in the chimney for thunder. Our old dog, Quince, was terrified in any storm and would crawl under my desk or onto my lap if I would let him.

I suppose we are all affected by our surroundings, even though we may not realize it until we leave them. When I am away from Maine I am uneasy and long for the mountains and the sea. People who live in the Rockies would not think much of our mountains; Katahdin, Maine's highest, is only 5,268 feet, and the one I look at, Western Mountain on Mount Desert Island, is but a modest fifth of that. All things, though, are relative. I view Western Mountain from not much above sea level, and I have lifted my eyes to a 12,000-foot peak in the Sierra Madre that seemed no more lofty—but I stood 11,000 feet up on the *alto plano.*

The thing that would most depress me if I had to leave here to live in a city would be the loss of intimate contact with the elements. I know that rain falls on cities, as it does on the country, and that in a city one sometimes sees dirty snow. I know that some days are colder and some are hotter than others, but there one experiences little personal involvement with weather conditions. In the country one lives *with* the weather, not as a citizen of a besieged fortress fighting against it.

Even worse than being compelled to live in a city would be to have to reside in one of the vast faceless stretches of suburbia surrounding one. There the trees do not grow where they will, as they do with us, but are regimented like slaves, and when their leaves fall they do not return to the soil to foster new growth but are hurried off by the Department of Sanitation lest they plug up the sewers.

143

If it snows or rains or is hot or cold, except within very narrow limits, the citizens of suburbia complain about the weather. Snow is inadmissible—except that it may whiten the grass and evergreen trees on Christmas Eve—and if you have ever tried to drive home to the suburbs during the rush hour after a two-inch snowfall, you know why. If it could be arranged, rain might be permitted to fall on the lawns and gardens at night, but not when anyone wanted to go shopping or visiting or to play golf.

As for temperature, a maximum of about eighty degrees and a minimum of about fifty would be all right. Of course, if the kids wanted to go swimming or skiing, something hotter or colder would be allowed, but it would have to be confined to where they were going and not upset the other inhabitants.

Those of us who live in the country take the weather as it comes. There is nothing we can do about it anyway, and not much that we would want to. It is a part of our life, always with us and always changing. We are not gathered together to deny its existence; we submit to its moods and enjoy them or put up with them. A snowfall of a few inches does not discommode us, and rain we ignore unless it is so heavy as to gully the land. We roll with the punches as do the wild things who live here with us.

When the snow gets deep in winter the deer gather together and yard up, keeping it trampled down, and browse on the surrounding cedars. When spring comes they step daintily out of the woods and feed on the fresh young grass at the edge of my hay field. They used to feed on my vegetables during the summer, but I fenced them out.

I saw a fox yesterday, trotting along in the rain, dragging his brush. Suddenly with one clear bound, he (it may have been a vixen—I am not knowledgeable about the sex of foxes) landed on top of a large boulder and sat there motionless, thinking foxy thoughts, probably planning his next visit to my hen house.

Late last fall, on the edge of winter, a bobcat worked its way across our patch of wild blueberries, slowly, cautiously, like the house cat that is at this moment mousing on the hillside outside my window. The bobcat was mousing too; they do not kill as many chickens and larger game as they are accused of. I saw it again on the road, one snowy afternoon, lifting its feet the way our yellow cat Butterscotch does, when it walks in the snow.

A number of weeks past, on a day of mild February thaw, a grouse exploded beside me from where it had been budding a roadside tree. This morning, after yesterday's storm had blown itself out, I walked around to see what damage had been done. I found a window broken in the guest house. A nine-by-twelve-inch pane had been shattered into at least 100 fragments and was scattered fifteen feet across the living room floor. Lying there among the shards of glass was a grouse. I can imagine that at the height of the gale it had become confused and flew headlong into the glass, seeking a haven from the storm.

The greatest blessing granted to those who live in the country is that they are still aware that man is but one character, and a not very important one (except to himself) in the whole scheme of things. If we were to vanish completely and utterly from the earth at one time, there would not even be a sigh to note our passing. We do pass, all of us, one by one, and in a generation or so are beyond the personal recall of any living man. If we are reminded of this occasionally it is humbling and useful to us. We are very proud of our civilization and we like to think we can organize and tabulate and control things, but we cannot even control a few puffs of wind that we call a "northeaster," and as far as nature is concerned, we are of no more consequence than the grouse that flew through the guest house window.

Wing High, Wing Low

My wife said to me as we went to bed last night, "I hope those peepers get out of their shells before the pond dries up!"

They will, I am sure, as they are the sort of peepers that have no feathers, those that my neighbors farther south call knee-deeps, which I think is an excellent name for them, for if you follow their song at this time of year you will soon be knee-deep in a swamp. Our pond is porous, it has holes in it, and when the general water table drops, the pond dries up and stays that way until the fall rains fill the ground with moisture once more. In the meantime the *Hylodes,* having concluded their nursery activities, will have migrated to more congenial surroundings.

I love to hear the peepers, for theirs is a true spring song, a love song. It never fails and never varies; it is an echo of the call of the Argonauts seeking Hylas, who was bewitched by the nymphs of the spring where he went to fetch water. I am not alone in my affection for them. Thoreau could be expected to be familiar with them during his long chilly walks around Concord in early spring, and he was, and remarked, *"Hylodes pickeringii,* a name that is longer than the frog itself!"

We associate peepers with the cold days of early spring, and rightly so, but there are other signs triggered by the same clock that we are not so apt to notice, because they are not noisy. One that is also aqueous in habitat is the skunk cabbage that pushes its purple horns above the ground to coincide with the first chorus of *Hylodes*.

Another early riser is the dogtooth violet, which grows a little higher above the water table than the skunk cabbage, but not much. There is one spot, beside the road to the shore, where their spotted leaves (which account for their sometimes being called trout lilies) appear by the thousand. There are never many of the nodding yellow flowers, so few in fact that I feel guilty about picking any, but I always do, for the plants generate by underground offsets, which is why they become so crowded. Actually, if one had time and energy it would be helpful to their flowering if they were thinned out occasionally because, like the human race, they multiply too rapidly.

A sound that is as springlike to me as the song of the peepers—but probably not considered so elsewhere—is the croaking of the ravens. We have a pair here that I think are resident. They do live year-round on the coast, but either because they are silent in winter or because I am not out so much to hear them, I associate them with spring. Theirs is a hoarse, contemptuous call, having nothing of affection about it. It is in the nature of a Bronx cheer to man, whose hand has always been against them. I heard the ravens today as I stood behind the barn where I was sheltered from the wind. They were flying high, with their great black wings spread wide, wing high, wing low, as they were buffeted from side to side by the gale. In the intervals between their croaking I could hear the constant humming of the wind in the power lines overhead.

When I was a boy I used to place my ear to the telegraph poles to see if I could distinguish the messages being transmitted along the wires, and when I was even younger I watched hopefully for the little envelopes to whiz along and wondered why I was never able to see one. Having grown old, I am no longer able to be intrigued by such mysteries—which is my loss—but today, making sure that no one was looking, I pressed my ear once more against the pole and found the music unchanged, though the players had been fiddling for more than half a century.

It was only a preview of spring, and soon over, so being chilled and a little sad, I came in by the fire to watch the scuds of misty rain drive in from the sea, and to think on all the earlier occupants of this old house who had seen winters move reluctantly into spring.

"Hundreds" of Scarlet Tanagers

Years ago, when I lived in Pennsylvania, a neighbor who was a very keen bird lady telephoned me one morning to ask, excitedly, if I had seen any scarlet tanagers. When I replied that I had seen only half a dozen in my life, she said, "Look out of your window into the orchard—there are hundreds of them." I did look and, if there were not hundreds, there were at least three or four black and scarlet birds among the apple blossoms. However, as the days passed, more came, and I saw a great many. It was the largest visitation of scarlet tanagers the area had ever experienced. Every morning, about the time I was shaving, Harriet would get me on the phone, soap all over my face, while she exultantly told me that this would be known as the year "that the tanagers were so bad."

But yesterday I came to the conclusion that this would be the year, around here anyway, that would be referred to as the year that the evening grosbeaks were so bad. We saw only a few all winter, but about three weeks ago they arrived in force and have been gobbling up sunflower seed as fast as I can replenish the feeder ever since. I have always welcomed them, for they are beautiful birds, and their bright yellow and white clothing is a cheerful contrast to the drab colors of winter. Usually they visit us in flocks of fifteen or twenty birds, stay awhile, and then disappear until the next lot shows up. Not so this year. When they came they deployed in platoon strength, up to sixty at a time, and stayed quarreling on the feeder from sunup to sunset. Their manners are deplorable. Not content with attacking each other, they do their best to drive off all other birds and succeed to the point where small citizens, like chickadees and pine siskins, can get only a mouthful, furtively. They even drive off cowbirds and starlings, which is something of an accomplishment.

Pine siskins are friendly little fellows but I think their exclusion from the feeders makes them even more tame. Yesterday, when I stepped onto the terrace wall to hang out a baitbag filled with suet, a pine siskin was perched on a twig only a couple of feet from me. He seemed completely unafraid, so I held out the bag toward him. He eyed me speculatively for ten or fifteen seconds and then, deciding that even if I was larger than a grosbeak I seemed less hostile, flew onto the suet and began to feed. In a few seconds he was joined by another, so that now, being cramped for space, he hopped onto my thumb and fed from there.

I suppose it is because wild things, generally, are fearful of human beings (and well they should be) that we gain such a sense of elation when one decides to trust us. The touch of those tiny wiry feet clutching my thumb gave me a remarkable sense of accomplishment. At the same time I was amazed by the lack of weight. I could see the bird and I could feel its feet, but it was as though a flower petal had fallen on my hand. It seemed impossible that anything so tiny could successfully brave the rigors of a Maine winter, and it made me realize how necessary a constant supply of fuel is to feed its metabolic processes.

The Bible tells us that "All flesh is as grass," and the needs of that little fluff of feathers are the same as my own. Fortunately we are not in competition, so I can view the birds (excluding the crows that steal my corn) without rancor. Though I take second place to no one in my love for the country, and my desire to keep it inviolate, I wonder if the way-out ecologists in their missionary zeal have not overlooked the fact that the dictionary (Webster's) defines ecology as "the branch of biology that deals with the relations between living organisms and their environment . . . " and does not carry any suggestion that it is something fixed, like the laws of the Medes and the Persians.

One gains the impression that some environmental enthusiasts would like to arrest all change, although if that were to be done it would seem consistent to freeze all social relationships too, for ecology also means ". . . the relationship between the distribution of human groups with reference to material resources and the consequent social and cultural patterns." I am afraid the less privileged people of the earth would view this with something less than enthusiasm. The reason that we Americans have the ability to grow vast amounts of wheat, to feed ourselves and others, is that we upset the ecology of the great Middle West. We burnt, and plowed, thousands of square miles of buffalo grass, and eliminated the buffalo in so doing. I doubt that even the most rabid ecologist would suggest that we put the land back into buffalo grass, nor do I believe one would find many supporters for changing all of America east of the Appalachians back into the "forest primeval" that existed when the white man first set foot on this continent four centuries ago.

Ecology is not, and never has been, static. It is a fluid, ever-changing condition, and while man has had something to do with the changes that have occurred, and are still occurring, there are far greater forces than *Homo sapiens* at work. What we can do, is avoid being more disturbing than is absolutely necessary. Meanwhile man will, in the final analysis, govern his actions by what he conceives to be his own self-preservation. Of that we can be sure.

Closer to my mind, though, is the necessity (my necessity) of keeping the deer and coons from raiding my garden. So to my way of thinking, if I disturb the ecology a little in the process I shall have to take the burden on my already sin-stained soul.

Contemplation

Everyone has to make peace, one way or another, with the everyday frustrations of existence. Some fail of any practical accommodation and opt out of the stream of life altogether, to spend their days doing nothing useful, like a dog chasing its own tail. Others struggle, living their lives bitter, baffled, and defeated; convinced, as a young man who should have known better once told me, that everything is a racket. Fortunately most of us, admitting that this is not the most perfect of all possible worlds, recognize that it is the only one we are likely to see, and so we decide we had better make the best of it.

Few men are so fortunate as to have been employed all their days at an occupation that filled every minute with an engrossing interest. For most of us, our employment is a way of making a living, rather than a whole life. While the former is ideal, the latter is not a hopeless alternative. What needs to be remembered is that living goes on in one's mind, and that under even the most trying of circumstances a richer and happier life can be had by working at it.

Henry Thoreau remarked that he "came into this world not chiefly to make this a good place to live in, but to live in it, good or bad," and when we get particularly exasperated with some unusually irritating idiocy, it is well to remember that we are not charged with correcting it. What we are charged with, when we come alone into this world, is to live our lives as best we may until the day when, once more alone, we go out of it.

What is certainly one of the saddest aspects of modern western civilization is the fact that the hours of freedom granted to man by modern technology are not being employed in living. We probably have twice as much leisure time as our grandparents had, but most of us allow it to slip through our hands unused.

I realize that everyone does not measure life by the same yardstick, and that as a gardener and countryman my viewpoint may differ from that of others; but my chief regret is that ever fewer people seem to learn the joys of tranquility. Last summer I took one of my visitors on a walk through the woods and along the shoreline. I showed him one of my favorite vantage points on a rocky outcrop, hemmed about by spruces but with a glorious view out across the bay. He expressed himself ecstatically, so I said, "Why don't you stay here? I have to go back to the house to be available for a telephone call." He thought that a wonderful idea, so I went about my business. I do not think I had been in the house ten minutes before I noticed him poking around in his car getting some maps, which he told me he needed to plan the rest of his trip. He was not leaving for three days!

Now, this same man would pay $10 to be allowed to sit for two hours to watch a baseball game or to listen to a concert, but could not sit for more than ten minutes alone with his own mind, even though his surroundings were as beautiful as a Brahms symphony.

As a gardener I get a deep satisfaction out of my avocation, though it is not only from planting and growing, interesting as that may be. The greatest fulfillment comes from contemplation. The early morning, when you leave behind you the imprint of your footsteps on the silver dew-covered lawn; high noon, when the crinkled petals of the poppies burst from the green paper envelopes that contain them; dusk, when the white trumpets of the tobacco open to the moths, and the fragrance drifts in waves on the quiet air.

Sunday

When I was a schoolboy, which candor compels me to tell you was a great many years ago, Sunday was a very special day. It was special for a number of reasons. To begin with it was the only day we had our big meal at two o'clock. On other days we dined at seven post meridian, on the dot. Also, Sunday was marked by the appearance of either roast beef, roast lamb, or roast chicken. I didn't think much of roast beef because I was made to eat the fat, which I considered to be slippery; and roast lamb sometimes also turned up on weekdays, so that roast chicken was in the way of being the *pièce de résistance*. The skin was always brown and crisp and, as has apparently been the custom since ancient times, small boys were given a drumstick. I delighted in the drumstick and still do. The low estate into which chicken has fallen in these latter days is sad to contemplate. The crowning glory of the meal, though, was the dessert. Nowadays kids would sniff at it, but I thought it wonderful. It was a fancy gelatin mold, usually lemon flavored, but sometimes, in season, raspberry or strawberry.

In the days that I speak of, gelatin—where I lived anyway—did not come out of a package but was made by boiling bones, calves feet by preference. To make good jelly was a job that took some little time and effort, which was, probably, the reason we only had it on Sunday. I can hear some of my readers saying: "Boiled bones. Ugh!" To them I would respond by asking what they think packaged gelatin is made from and, when they answer that they do not know, informing them that it is bones. I have seen many a cargo of them, odoriferous in the warm summer sunshine, being unloaded from a ship that had carried them from an Argentine slaughterhouse for delivery to an American gelatin manufacturer.

But I really did not intend to talk about bones, but about the decay of Sunday. The other thing I miss about the old-fashioned Sunday is its atmosphere, the Sundayishness of the day, that has vanished with the years. When I was young nobody, except a few who were engaged in critical occupations, worked on the Sabbath. Critical occupations, in the country, included milking the cows that know nothing about resting on the seventh day and, in the cities, keeping the public utilities operating. Generally, though, Sunday was a day of rest. The Presbyterians even supported an organization called "The Lord's Day Alliance" that was dedicated to the abolition of work on Sundays. No shops were open except perhaps the corner store, for an hour, to sell the Sunday newspaper, and they were considered by good Christian folk to be flirting with the Devil. Not a few families, particularly the Methodists, arranged their affairs so that they did not even have to cook on Sundays. They did their cooking for the weekend on Saturday. While the matriarch of the household sheltered herself behind the Biblical injunction against working on the Sabbath, I suspect her piety was not uninfluenced by a feeling that she was entitled to a day off anyway.

Sunday morning was busy. Everyone had to be up and away to Sunday school and church, and by the time that was over and they were back at home, the morning was spent. I cannot recall that I felt particularly put upon by being made to attend Sunday school. All my friends, or most of them, were compelled to do likewise. Even the Catholics (fearsome sect in those days) attended Sabbath rites (that I thought probably had something to do with the agonies of Maria Monk, the heroine of a book residing behind the locked glass doors of my grandfather's bookcase). I did envy them being able to dispose of their religious obligations early in the morning, thus having the greater part of the day off. They were not held as strictly to account for their personal activities on Sunday, after they had attended church, as were we Protestants.

On the whole, though, Sunday was a pretty good day. Even though I had to attend morning service, and bob up and down at the appropriate moments, I did not have to listen to the sermon. All I had to do was to keep quiet and *don't fidget*. I can still see the long shafts of sunlight shining diagonally from the upper windows across the pews and hear the buzzing of an occasional bee whose apian mind was unimpressed by the rule of silence. I could wonder where one would arrive if one could scale the sunbeam, like Jack climbing the beanstalk; and in reverse, what a terrific ride one would have could one slide down it and be deposited in front of the pulpit. Then there was always the fond hope, never realized, that the bee would sting the preacher.

After church we went home to a stupendous meal which, accompanied by a bottle of wine that my grandfather shared parsimoniously with my grandmother (and even more frugally with me), guaranteed me a free afternoon. Grandmother disappeared upstairs until about four o'clock. Grandfather leaned back in his chair, read a few paragraphs of the newspaper, and then placed it over his face and went to sleep. I was at liberty to do what I pleased as long as I did not get dirty or make noise. As the house was filled with books and I was an omnivorous reader (radio and television not yet having been invented), I never lacked for amusement. I knew where the key to the locked bookcase was hidden so that, if I cared to, I could read Maria Monk or shudder at the gruesome photographs of suffering humanity displayed in the pages of Foote's *Minor Surgery.* Strange as it may seem to modern kids I also read the Bible for pleasure. Naturally, I knew where to find all the dirty bits about "he who pisseth against a wall," but I also developed an affection for the glorious and stately phrases of Elizabethan English that made it possible for me to enjoy Shakespeare in later years when most of my contemporaries hated him because they had never learned to march to the cadence of his music.

Sunday, in these latter days is, for most people, a nothing. It does not even have much significance as a day on which they do not have to go to work because nobody works on Saturday, either. It is not a day of rest but a day that is like any other day. Mammoth marts, and the like, are open and crowded. Highways are jammed with cars, and if you want chicken for dinner you stand in line in the gasoline-tainted air and buy it from the Colonel, and then eat it with your hands while sitting in your car. Grandfather, who folded his napkin, starched and white as the driven snow, even after he had patted his mustache with it, and replaced it in its heavy silver ring, would not have approved.

Perhaps we were not as emancipated, nor as traveled, because one could not then take one's numbered seat in an aluminum box and be hurled across the Atlantic in a few hours, to arrive in exactly the same idiot society that one had left. We could not watch professional sports because there were no televisions or announcers to tell us what we were watching. We could not go for a ride in an automobile because they were scarce, and viewed with suspicion. We did not know at that time that the internal combustion engine would be responsible for laying waste half the civilization our ancestors had created. Strangely though, we survived, and three-quarters of a century later the young, *mirabile dictu,* are discovering, as though they were Magellan circumnavigating the globe, that happiness is to be found at home, in simple things.

154

Happiness

I wrote once, at the not inconsiderable risk of being thought "square," that I was a happy man. It is not the vogue, today, to be happy. One constantly hears or reads about unhappiness. We are told of international crises, of terrorists, of muggings, rapes, robberies, arson, murders or attempted murders (including heads of governments by heads of other governments). We are admitted to confessions of immorality by high elected officials. The world, it seems, is in bad shape. No one is decent, no one is honest, and if you do not agree you are a Pollyanna.

I suppose most would say I am happy because I have a beautiful wife, own a beautiful house with a beautiful garden, live in a beautiful part of the country free from alarums, and have enough money. What is "enough" is variable. Thoreau said the way to wealth was by not wanting too much. Yes, I admit these blessings help but I have not always enjoyed them, in spite of which I have always been—except for brief intervals—a happy man.

The truth is that happiness, though aided by fortunate circumstances, does not dwell in them. It makes its home in the mind. My favorite Roman philosopher, Marcus Aurelius Antoninus (I did not view him with such affection when I had to construe his Latin as a schoolboy), remarked "No man is happy who does not think himself so."

I was lucky enough to be born in the country, and stayed there and in the small country town where I went to school, until I was a young man and went off to war. When the war was over, and by a miracle I was still alive, I had to enter into the work of the world in order to support myself. Like most others I did not have any money, and no access to any, and I learned quickly that there is nothing like an empty belly to sharpen a man's enthusiasm for gainful employment. I worked in many parts of the world, both on land and on sea.

I discovered that even though I had not inherited money I had been given something far more valuable, an affection for rural life and, best of all, an appreciation of the small, pleasant, daily incidents of life there. Happiness is woven of an accumulation of seemingly trivial events. It is like manna from heaven, fresh every day for the gathering. I learned not to trample it underfoot while searching for more spectacular miracles.

I was fortunate, too, in having had what is somewhat scornfully spurned today as a classical education. In my day it was the norm. It did not confer upon one any specific skill calculated to increase one's future income—that knowledge was acquired elsewhere, at a university if one was headed for medicine, the law, teaching, or the church; at a trade school or business if that was the direction in which one's talents lay.

The purpose of a secondary education in those days was to broaden the mind, to inculcate logical thinking, to teach the student to express his ideas with clarity; in short, to equip him to be a useful, thoughtful adult. He had, of course, acquired the basic tools of reading, writing, and arithmetic in elementary school.

I doubt that most high school students today (or college students, either) are well acquainted with English literature. In earlier times schoolmasters, no matter what their specific subject, used literary allusions in their teaching and expected their students to respond with understanding. One of my masters left in my memory a few lines from Pope's "Ode on Solitude":

> *Happy the man whose wish and care*
> *A few paternal acres bound,*
> *Content to breathe his native air*
> *In his own ground.*

I had no paternal acres but wherever I journeyed around the world those lines remained with me, and I thought of them as expressing my greatest desire. Money or fame or worldly success I did not expect, but I hoped that someday I could settle where I could gather the grains of happiness I saw all about me. Somewhere in the country.

I rise by the sun these summer days which means between five and six o'clock. When I come downstairs into the little vestibule that old Maine houses have just inside the front door, the early light shines through the narrow windows flanking it. The sun is rising over the offshore islands and shadows lie long across the grass. Morning light is as different from evening light as white wine is from red.

When I open the door there is no sound but the wind or the gulls or, perhaps, the farm noises of roosters, sheep, or cattle. The road past my house is little used, except by my neighbors, who are mostly lobstermen and clammers. The lobstermen are at work by five o'clock. The clammers' hours of work are governed by the tides.

Sometimes there is a silver haze across the water. Sometimes the water is blue and flecked with whitecaps. Sometimes it is as still and calm as gray eternity. Sometimes I cannot see beyond my pasture fence because the fog rolls into the house when I open the door. I am overwhelmed by beauty—and happiness.

A Guide Down East

Some years ago a friend gave me a large outdoor thermometer. It is circular and eighteen inches in diameter, and is fastened to a wall where I can read it from my library window. My friend said it would serve me when I grew old and my eyesight failed. I have no doubt it will, as the figures, white on a black background, are two inches tall. At the moment, high noon, it registers eighty degrees which, if it were correct, would be hot for coastal Maine. It is, however, overly enthusiastic, as a more accurate mercurial instrument hung below it certifies to only seventy-five degrees. During the summer I am quick to point out this discrepancy to my visitors, but in winter I remain silent because when the true temperature is zero the large instrument records ten below—and around here we all like to boast about sub-zero cold and the wind-chill factor.

It interests me that the natives complain more about the length of the winter and its cold than do those of us who are from away. They are, on the other hand, less critical of hot summer days than are we. I suppose, having spent a good part of my life (in the days before air conditioning) in Philadelphia, a city noted for its heat and humidity, I am content to put up with a few months of cold in return for comfort in the summer. The tropics hold no fears for Philadelphians, as their city's reputation for blistering summer heat is world famous.

Maine, A Guide Down East, a product of the Federal Writers Project of the WPA, describes the state as enjoying a healthful and invigorating climate with summer heat less than that of New York or Massachusetts by about 32 percent. The truth of this statement is confirmed each year by reports of temperatures in the nineties in those states to the south of us, and is the reason Bar Harbor was sought out by the rich, and flourished in the horse-and-buggy days. Though it is now but a shabby tourist town, the climate remains as delightful as ever—though if you want to see the flowers for which its gardens were once famous, you have to go elsewhere on the island—Seal Harbor and Northeast Harbor, for instance, where the old Bar Harbor summer residents joined their friends after the 1947 fire.

A Guide Down East describes Bar Harbor as "the center of social and commercial life on the island. In summer the two business streets are lined with small shops, branches of those on Fifth and Madison avenues in New York, and are filled with brightly dressed visitors and summer residents." This may have been true in 1937, when the *Guide* was published, and even more so twenty years earlier, but today the fine stores have been replaced by tawdry gift and linen emporiums and the narrow sidewalks are crowded with tourists clothed in the peculiar summer garb of today that emphasizes obesity, large bosoms, and overdeveloped derrières.

It appears, informality being the order of the day, that people are convinced they cannot enjoy themselves unless they are attired in apparel better suited to a circus than to the street, and the less of it the better. While I have no objection to seeing pretty girls and handsome boys with little on (in appropriate surroundings), I think it behooves the elder citizens (and not too old in many cases) to keep their rarely attractive bodies discreetly out of sight.

I yearn, hopelessly I know, for a return to the fashions of yesteryear when ladies on holiday dressed themselves in crisp cool cotton or linen and peeked at you demurely (but with sparkling eyes) from under the wide brims of beautiful hats. I pine, also, for a return to seersucker suits and Panama hats for men. Such attire is far more attractive than hairy, sweaty chests revealed by half-open "Hawaiian" shirts draped over purple shorts that fail to cover knobby knees and skinny legs. I am also given to wonder at the attraction of sandals (discarded by Central Amerian Indians as soon as they can afford shoes), which have gained such favor as an article of summer attire. A young man once told me that feet—presumably female feet—were sexy. I answered that if he were to elevate his sights a bit, his reward would be greater.

But there, I am an old man who enjoys tea and little cucumber sandwiches at four in the afternoon and likes the company of ladies, young or old, who wear pretty dresses, which give me an opportunity to use my imagination about what is underneath. I was always given to understand that fantasies were the stuff that dreams are made of—"half revealing, half concealing"—but it seems now that nothing but the naked truth will suffice, no matter how unattractive it may be.

Mullein Days

Easily the most spectacular plants in my garden these August days are the mulleins. I am amazed that they are not better known—almost the first question I am asked by visitors is, "What is that beautiful, tall yellow flower?"

I live in a house by the side of the road but I don't watch the race of men go by. One reason is that I do not have time, and the other is that they do not go by, they come in. The mulleins toll them in. (We call decoys "tollers" in these parts.) When I tell people what they are, they look puzzled because they think of the roadside mullein with its tiny flowers and generally scrawny appearance, so I unleash the plant's botanical name, *Verbascum*, which better accords with its dignity.

The common mullein, which inhabits run-out fields and roadsides, is *Verbascum thapsus,* one of our less desirable aliens that slipped in from Europe without a passport. Even it, though, is not to be wholly despised, for although its flowers are nothing, its large woolly leaves are most attractive when covered with fog or dew. I am told that the wool once was used for lamp wicks, but it must have been a job to collect.

The plant that graces my garden is *Verbascum olympicum,* or at least I think it is. I am not sure, for the *Verbascums* are loose livers and great cuckolds, so it well may carry the bar sinister. In any event it is the most beautiful of the tribe that I have ever seen. My original plant, long gone, came from a nursery in Bar Harbor but its descendants, like the tribes of Israel, have spread far and wide. It is a biennial, which means that the seedlings that grow this year will bloom the next and then die. All I do now is weed out the hundreds I do not want, and if some have failed to spring up where I want them, I move a few in from elsewhere, as they transplant readily.

In their first year mulleins produce a basal rosette of great hairy leaves. In the second season a stem as thick as a walking stick grows as fast as Jack's beanstalk and, by the time the flowers show, is six feet tall. In addition to the central stalk, as many as twenty additional ascending stems develop from the bottom, all covered with two-inch, single yellow flowers. Each flower lasts only a day but they continue in profusion for weeks. With us they commence to bloom in July before the delphiniums have passed, and make the most arresting combination in the garden. There is also a white variety named after Miss Wilmott, a famous amateur gardener who lived in England. It differs only in the color of its flowers. It does not appear to self-seed as readily as the yellow, so we are going to try to save a few seeds.

In addition to all its other virtues mullein is the only plant that is almost storm-proof. I suppose a hurricane could knock one down but I can say that I have never seen it happen; the stalk was bent, perhaps, but never down. All the flowers may be blown off but the next day it will be arrayed again in all its glory. It has only contempt for weather that turns petunias and most other annuals into a soggy, mildewed, unhappy mess. When the fog blows in from the bay and stays week after week, as it has done this year, the flowers of the mullein are wider and brighter than ever. We call foggy days "mullein days." The only days that *Verbascums* dislike are those when the temperature climbs and the sun burns down out of a brassy sky. Then the flowers will fold in on themselves and look like the common roadside mullein, but in the cool of the evening, when the sun has gone down, they open wide again.

There are other *Verbascums,* both biennial and perennial, that have been developed in England, in other colors. They are attractive but do not have the statuesque character of *V. olympicum* and do not seem to be blessed with its generally rugged nature. The best of them are the Cotswold hybrids: Cotswold Beauty, which is bronze; Cotswold Gem, terra cotta; Cotswold Queen, salmon; and Pink Domino, mauve-pink. These are all shorter plants, up to three feet, and are worth having—but they won't lure passing travelers in off the road like *V. olympicum.*

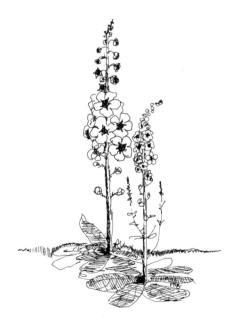

The Land

When I walked down the lane this morning I noticed that Cindy Too had been reaching through the fence to crop the foliage of the wild cherries and apples growing in the hedgerow. Cows, like humans, think the grass on the other side of the road is greener, but if they have enough to eat in the pasture their forays are more in the nature of a small boy stealing apples than a serious attempt to feed. Cindy Too and her pasture mate, a boarder, had been pushing hard at the fences and we soon discovered that they were not just having a good time but were really hungry. A couple of bales of hay were soon disposed of and proved the point.

The rains of the last few weeks have brought the young grass thrusting through the old dry growth, which we mowed off not long ago, but there is not enough of it to satisfy the cattle. Feeding out a little hay, even though it's early to be ravishing the haymow, will carry them along until they get a good bite. I like to keep them out as long as possible, not only to save hay but because the longer they can get green feed, the better they will winter.

We have kept a few cows as long as we have lived here. Certainly there is no economical excuse for doing so but it grieves me to see the fields that our ancestors labored so hard to clear, going back to brush. If you have a few acres of cleared land, the cost of keeping a cow is trifling. Even if you do not milk her, a veal calf once a year is a good return, and if you are a gardener you know the value of barn dressing.

When I first came here to live we were able to arrange for artificial insemination and had our choice from a number of registered bulls of several breeds. Nowadays, the call for breeding is so small that the plan has had to be abandoned in this area, and were it not for the cooperation of a neighbor who lends me his bull, we would be unable to breed our animals. We could, of course, keep our own bull but that is not very practical when you have only a couple of heifers.

My neighbor's willingness to bring his bull on a fifty-mile round trip to keep my small operation going is a labor of love. The stud fee is insignificant. He goes to the trouble because he loves the land and hates to see it growing up to alders. When I looked out of the window the other day he was there by the barn with his pedigreed Guernsey bull in a little pickup truck. The bull is a quiet young animal, two years old, and just barely fits in the truck—his hind end hangs over the tailgate. He was very unexcited about his mission. He backed down a little ramp, walked sedately across the road, accomplished what he was brought for, and in five minutes was led back by his halter to the truck, which he walked right into as though glad to get the job done and be on his way home.

I talked to his owner about how sad it is that so little use is now being made of the land. Fifty years ago family cows were commonplace, and people living in small towns like my own often kept a pig or two as well, and all had gardens. We talk a lot about people who are starving, about pollution, and about the changing ecology, but not much is really being done about it. What is being done is on a governmental level. People seem to have lost their desire for independent action and personal accomplishment. Not many years ago this land we live on supported a lot of people who took care of themselves. Perhaps they did not own two cars and three television sets, but they thought their own thoughts and ran their own affairs. Pollution in those days was on a scale that the environment could absorb without difficulty, and ecological change was at a rate that the world had lived with for millennia.

Admittedly, individuals cannot do much about lessening industrial pollution, except by banding together, because industrial pollution is caused by enormously wealthy corporations with paid lobbyists in every legislature, whose sole objective is to defeat any action that will lessen the profit made by their employers. On the other hand, there are many things that we can do individually, matters involving persistent poisonous sprays and other chemicals, waste and sewage disposal, and reclamation of the land which, though small individually, are enormously important collectively. By personal involvement we strengthen our own determination and present a stronger front to the despoilers.

Perhaps my neighbor's handsome young bull, doing his part to maintain some of the virtues of the old order, is sowing seed that will make for a saner world far outside the boundaries of my small stony pasture.

A Message from Maine

Dear Alden:

You asked me to give you a periodic report on your building operation. I have just returned from Carter's Point, and the first thing I want to tell you is that you have chosen the most beautiful place in the world in which to live. I don't mean Carter's Point particularly, although that is lovely enough; what I really mean is coastal Maine, east of Portland. I exclude the coast west of Portland; that has become merely a suburb of Boston. I know I really don't have to tell you this, as your forebears lived in Maine for 200 years, but since you have been away for a long time, you will forgive an adopted son for bragging about your country.

When I got up this morning the sky was banked with heavy clouds and the temperature stood at forty-eight degrees, a mite chilly, but a light wool shirt made it comfortable. I used to think that high black clouds presaged rain but I have learned that here they often mean just wind. When the wind came, driving away the clouds, the heavens turned to cobalt and the sun shone.

I dropped Helen off at Blue Hill, on my way, and was happy to note that there were only about a dozen cars in town. There weren't many people either, and I recognized those that were, a sign that the tidal wave of summer is ebbing. I am sorry the tourists and the summer people miss the two best months of the year, September and October, but my grief is assuaged by my knowledge that the pace of life here will soon slow down to about what it was when Henry Ford introduced the Model A.

It is not autumn yet but the year is winding down. The swallows are gone and the robins are thinning out. When the last migrating robins go south they will strip the berries from my rowan trees. I guess the berries are not ripe enough for the first migrants, but later travelers take on a full cargo. The fields and roadsides are splashed with color, mostly goldenrod and fall asters, gold and lavender. When I passed Tom Schroth's place I saw a couple of wild asters blooming in the ditch. One was pinker than any I have and I debated whether to acquire it larcenously or to ask if I might dig it. He probably hasn't noticed that it is different and would not miss it, but I think I shall ask for it and thus feel more righteous when I fulminate about wild flower vandals.

Though the maples have not yet turned, there is an amazing amount of color. A few days ago we were riding a visitor from Mexico around and, as she saw one tree after another bearing red fruit, she wanted to know what they were. When, finally, we stopped to identify one it turned out to be a wild apple but then, pretty soon, she saw something else and that was a rowan tree; and a little later when she exclaimed over a group of shrubs that brightened the roadside they were our lovely fragile wild roses, burdened with orange hips. Here and there we passed hedges of Rugosa roses unbelievably heavily laden with brilliant red fruit. Those you saw in my garden, Alden, now have hips an inch-and-a-half in diameter, like small apples. I have been picking some to make rose hip jelly. Rugosa roses grow so well here that most people think they are native, but they are not, not to Maine, anyway. They came from Japan but, like a lot of other immigrants, are enormously appreciative of their surroundings.

Just before I crossed Carlton Stream I saw a crew collecting hay. One man was riding an ancient tractor, which was coughing its way uncertainly across the uneven field, dragging an old horse rake, while the others were throwing the hay onto a pickup truck. I stopped to watch them for a while. Their predecessors in ownership had gathered hay in the same way a century ago. The motive power was different then, horses instead of gasoline engines, but everything else was the same. I am pretty sure that the hay was better in those days; the stuff being raked now was full of weedy trash and would not have made fodder, but was adequate for what it was going to be used for, burning off blueberry fields. Most fields, these days, are seared with kerosene burners but I enjoy seeing it done in the old way with the little flames flickering across the fields, and the smoke curling up and away with the wind.

When I reached the top of the hill I could look down across Salt Pond and see the rafts where my young friend Mark Richmond is raising oysters. Hard work and not much profit—none for a few years—but he is young and has time on his side, and what a way to make a living! Nonpolluting, nondepleting, nondestructive, nonoppressive. Fresh air, sunshine, rain, frost, snow, fog, wind, all of nature. He will never be a millionaire but he will never have to be ashamed of what he did to the world he lives in.

Climbing the next hill, by Punch Bowl Farm, I noticed that the enormous old barn had sagged a little more since I last saw it and I wondered how long it would be before it collapsed. To build such a barn today would involve more than any farmer in these parts could afford, and to repair it would be even more expensive. Like the old schooners lying on their beam ends at Wiscasset, it has lived beyond its time and cannot earn a living in this modern world where only efficiency has currency.

But about your house. I had forgotten. I coasted down the long hill into Sedgwick Village, in order to save gas, and passed only one car, the mailman's. You will be glad to learn that Route 175 has been resurfaced, but I was on it only a couple of minutes before I turned into your road. It, you will be even more happy to know, is as rough as ever, although the ditch that scored it diagonally from side to side at one point has been filled. Too smooth roads mean too many sightseers.

When I reached your house two men, who were leaning over the edge of the roof at what appeared to me to be an extremely hazardous angle, were nailing trim. One of them, who missed a nail, said "God damn it" when it bent, and then leaned out even farther to pull and replace it. You can still get honest work done around here. He did not just wham the nail home and trust to the paint to hide a botched job. Another man, who once worked for me, hailed me out of the blankness of an unfinished upper window, saying, "How do you think the fishing will be?" He was pointing to what you hope will someday be a pond. I replied that I thought it might be passable after the pond had gathered a little more water, and that it had a clay bottom which should hold whatever collected. My acquaintance agreed, and added that there should be plenty of water eventually, as the place was a swamp. My guess is that after the hole fills and the water clears, you will be able to catch your breakfast trout off your back porch.

You are getting a good house, Alden. It should be all buttoned in before snow flies, so the boys will be able to work under cover during the winter. It will probably cost you more than you can afford but you couldn't go broke in a better place. With prices going up every day, and the world becoming more confused and lawless month by month, Carter's Point is going to be a fair location to duck down behind the weather-cloth, as we did when we were at sea, and ride out the blow. You can have trout for breakfast, shoot a deer in the alders when it comes down to drink, and there is a level spot to make a garden. Besides, you won't be bothered by refugees from the cities to the south. When the sub-zero winds of the reach begin to blow up their pants legs in November, it will cool their ardor for rural life.

Hurry back before I eat all that rose hip jam. As ever,

Roy

Autumn's Sweet Sorrow

For many people autumn is tinged with sadness. The summer is over and gone, and soon the early frosts will strike down the more tender flowers and foretell the long winter to come. I suppose all of us are sorry to be reminded of the passage of time, particularly as the years accumulate, but it is a bitterness that leaves a trace of sweetness in the mind. From now until the year dies in the flaming foliage of October there will be a steady multiplication and change of color in nature's garden, which is there for us to enjoy if we take time to admire it.

Personally, I have always felt that the sadness in autumn was more wistful than depressing and, having been a gardener for so many years, have learned that there is never any end to anything, only change. Spring has its glory of freshness and rebirth, but fall brings completion and fulfillment.

Many years ago, in a Philadelphia bookshop, I found an old and tattered little volume entitled simply, *Emblemes,* authored by Francis Quarles, who was born in 1592 and died in 1644. He composed a number of poems on religious subjects and was well thought of in the seventeenth century. His books went into many editions. The copy that I cherish was published in 1684, long after his death, and authorities at Harvard tell me it is at least the twelfth edition. I must confess that I did not buy the book for reasons of piety, but because I was taken by the charm of some of his lines, and the reason I refer to Quarles now is that I want to share them with you. Toward the end of his book, Quarles devotes a poem to each decade of a man's life, and the one from which I quote is the sixth. He heads it "Yet a little while is the Light with you," which is a bit discouraging for those of us who have passed beyond that magic meridian. It goes:

> *And now the cold Autumnal dews are seen*
> > *To cobweb every green;*
> *And by the low-shorn Rowins doth appear*
> > *The fast declining year:*
> *The sapless branches doff their summer suits*
> > *And wain their winter fruits;*
> *And stormy blasts have forced the quaking trees*
> > *To wrap their trembling limbs in suits of mossy freez.*

In another volume of Quarles entitled *Enchiridion* there is a picture of the author, wearing a fine Cavalier haircut and a goatee. A handsome man. While I cannot determine from his picture whether I should have enjoyed his company, I can tell from his writing that he was a sensitive and observant person. More than 330 autumns have faded into winter since the *Emblemes* were written, but still the cold autumnal dews are seen to cobweb every green, and my rowans are ready to wain their winter fruits, even if they are not yet leafless.

The approach of autumn is made visible by other things besides the coloring of the fruits of the mountain ash. As the year runs down, the yellows and rusty browns and reds begin to dominate the landscape. The seed heads of the ripening grasses are changing from yellow to puce, as you look across them toward the afternoon sun. The chrome and gold of the *Solidagos,* the goldenrods—there are more than 100 species—are staining the fields and roadsides. The New England asters, with their purple flowers, golden centered—many of which will be with us until hard frost—are beginning to open their buds. Here and there a maple is turning red and yellow ahead of the big show which is several weeks away. When a maple tree or a branch of one assumes its autumn colors early, you can be sure it has suffered an injury, and if you take the trouble to look you will easily discover it.

When I walked down the lane to the shore this morning, I found the jewelweed, *Impatiens,* taking over from the fireweed, *Epilobium.* I suppose we call these lovely things weeds because we cannot domesticate them, but there are few cultivated flowers in my garden more beautiful. Nothing could be more dainty than the jewelweed with its pendulous flowers swaying to every breath of air; and the fireweed, which is now shedding its petals, has only just begun its show, for the long narrow seed pods will turn purple and last for weeks until, finally dry, they will twist and discharge the flossy, milkweed-like seeds on the autumn air.

No, I do not think the autumn sad. It arouses in me a nostalgia for other days, but that is a sweet sadness, and one that I can bear. In a few more weeks, when the leaves come down, the harsh cry of the blue jay will be heard, and the enameled lapis of his wings seen through the open branches of the trees. The dark green of the spruces will stand out sharply against the blue waters of the bay and, if you keep out of the wind, the sun will be warm on your back as you kneel to your task in the garden.

Summer's End

For the last two days we have been watching an easterly gale move up the coast (such are the blessings of television), and when I awoke this morning I knew by the sound of the wind moaning through the cracks around my bedroom windows that it had arrived. I leave the windows not quite closed because I like to be reminded of the high whistle that blows constantly through the rigging of a ship at sea. Our Victorian grandparents, who had a taste for such things, used to place a pretty toy called an Aeolian harp outside their windows—a little box over which were stretched a few tuned strings, a violin to be played by the wind.

These autumn days the eastern sky does not show much light before six o'clock, but by then the weather had moved in even though there was not yet any rain. The clouds were lowering and most of the birds were grounded. The sky met the water about a mile offshore so that I could not see Western Mountain, my usual forecaster of local weather conditions. We all knew we had better batten down. Even the sheep hung around their fold, a shelter that they have ignored all summer, and Cindy Too stayed by the barred gate where we have been feeding out a little hay because the pasture has been getting snug of late.

By noon the birches were tossing wildly and great curtains of rain, drifting in from the sea, beat against the windows of the house and passed on across the hay field behind it. The ventilators in the greenhouse rattled as though they would part company with the rest of the building and I went there to check them every half hour. They held, though, as they have done through many another storm. I comforted myself with the thought that it was not cold and there was nothing in there to freeze anyway. There have been winter storms when I have stayed up most of the night, though what I could have done had anything carried away, I do not know.

Although it will be some weeks yet before we drink our afternoon tea in front of the fire by lamplight, the days begin to draw in, and with the storm it was dark by five. The house felt warm and comfortable and I could sympathize with our puppy who, as I opened the door to take her out into the gale, took one startled look and fled back between my legs into the kitchen.

When we went to bed the wind was still howling and the rain driving by in sheets but the next morning, though nimbus clouds dragged their skirts across the bay, the western horizon was clear and, as the day passed, the sun shone and the breeze shifted into the west.

I spent all day clearing away the wreckage in the garden. Although there had been no frost, summer was over, and I knew there would not be enough left of autumn for the flowers to recover. The summer has gone out in a Gotterdammerung, the flames being supplied by the scarlet of the maples which have, this last week, set fire to the surrounding woodland.

The next day at sunset, while I was in the greenhouse, I heard the trumpeting of geese. I could hear their music distinctly but could not at first find them. Presently, looking into the west where dark clouds were banked before the setting sun, I discovered them. There they were, a thin angular line, high, high above the clouds in the cold light. I could distinguish nothing but a wavering thread, but even when they were almost lost in the fire of the sunset I could still hear their musical calling.

Though frost will come soon, and the geese are gone, there will be soft days yet to remind us that the year turns slowly upon its axis. We are but at the edge of autumn, and like the last years of a man's life, the days still to come may be the sweetest, perhaps because winter lies ahead.

Recycling

I think that farmers—gardeners in particular, and country people in general—are conscious that they live in a closed world. They see in their daily vocation, or avocation, that in nature nothing is ever wasted, that it is endlessly reused—recycled is the word that environmentalists have for it nowadays. They act as though recycling was something that man had invented and they are making a sacrifice by reusing beer cans and soda pop bottles instead of discarding them along the roadside.

In my garden nothing is ever wasted. If I grow more than I and my friends can eat, the excess goes to the hens who recycle it into eggs or to the cow who recycles it into milk and a veal calf.

The hens have first call on the lettuce that has run to seed, the pea haulms, and overripe cabbage. The cow gets the corn that the coons have beaten me to by twenty-four hours, and also the enormous zucchini that remain hidden under the leaves until I fall over them. Anything the animals do not want winds up in the compost heap, or is turned under where it grew, to decay and enrich the soil for next year.

Even the old wild apple trees the birds have planted make their contribution. The mice eat the fruit that falls to the ground; the grouse eat the seeds when the fruit has rotted or dried; and any apples that hang onto the tree into winter (as many do) are carried off by the crows.

Not even the feces of the animals, wild or domestic, is wasted. The birds of the air and the beasts of the field return their portion to the ground, and the cow manure (barn dressing in these parts) is hoarded by the gardener for re-use. The hen manure, being high in nitrogen, is spread on the sawdust that mulches the blueberries because, if it were not, the sawdust as it rotted would take nitrogen from the soil and starve the plants. It is mixed, too, with compost that is deficient in nitrogen.

Nothing is too small, or too large, to fit into this endless chain of birth, fruition, death, and re-use. The woods are burnt and nothing remains but gaunt black skeletons, but the potash from their burning feeds the drifts of purple fireweed that shelter the seedling poplars and alders. Presently will come the fir, the spruce, and the hardwoods again. Nothing has been added or subtracted, only changed.

Man is the only destroyer. In the western world, where most of the so-called advanced nations live, he even flushes his excreta wastefully away. It could and should be converted to fertilizer wherever sewage treatment plants operate. We even bury our dead six feet underground in a concrete box to guarantee they will be forever useless. Our ancestors did better. They wrapped their dead decently and set them to rest in a plain pine box in a shallow grave where in a few years they were recycled once the coffin rotted and the earth subsided—as a visit to any old country graveyard will testify.

When we speak of ourselves as an advanced nation, we do not think of the quiet villages and small towns. We don't consider the lobstermen hauling their traps, or the lights in the cow barns on dark winter mornings, the country roads, or the white-steepled churches. We equate "advanced" with thousands of miles of macadam highway, with enormous factories and gigantic cities, with thousands of acres of concrete runways, with power grids and oil refineries. We confuse material things (almost anything so long as it is big or there is a lot of it) with an advanced state of civilization.

Our obsession with size and speed and more of everything has led us into strange errors. We believe man has achieved a higher degree of civilization if he owns a color television rather than one that is black and white; if he has two radios instead of one; if he can drive at 70 mph instead of 50; if he burns oil instead of wood or coal; if he can set his thermostat at 72 instead of 68. (I am glad I am not in England to hear my friends go into gales of laughter because Americans think they are roughing it with their houses at 68.)

Apart from the temporary unemployment that may result from the energy crisis, it is probably the best thing that has happened to us in the last fifty years. There need be no permanent unemployment, for there is an infinity of useful, nondestructive, nonpolluting work to be done. Surely we are intelligent enough not to allow ourselves to be caught up in a belief that we have to keep making things which are useless and destructive of both the world's resources and our own welfare, in order to keep people employed.

What the energy crisis is saying to us is that we are galloping hell-bent in the wrong direction, that we should stop and look about us and realign and readjust our mode of life to accommodate itself to the realities. There is an old political proverb that says you can't buck city hall. Well, maybe. I don't know, but what I do know is that you can't buck nature. Work with her, yes. Guide her, sometimes. Ravage her and get away with it indefinitely, no.

Barbara Ward, wife of Sir Robert Jackson, a senior consultant at the United Nations, is reported by the *Christian Science Monitor* as calling attention to the fact that only a third of the world's present population is part of the technological age. She goes on to ask what would happen if the 7 billion expected by the year 2000 tried to live as extravagantly as the Europeans, Japanese, and Americans do now.

Two cars, television sets, supermarkets, antiperspirants, squeezable toilet paper (what does one do with toilet paper anyway to make its squeezability so important?), snowmobiles, humidifiers and dehumidifiers, throwaway beer cans, even throwaway babies under the new abortion laws, throwaway everything. How stupid can man be?

Gifts of the Garden

Not long ago, when a silver moon flickered across the waters of the bay, my elderly lady friends who are devotees of *The Old Farmer's Almanac* began to call to warn me there would be a frost. Most of my lady friends nowadays are elderly, which is not their fault. It is due to the fact that they were born about the same time I was, so we have grown old together. In addition to age they seem to have something else in common and that is a belief in words of country wisdom, one of these being that the first frost of autumn comes on the night of a full moon. Well, sometimes it does if the full moon happens to coincide with the first frost but, if it does, the moon has nothing to do with it. Frost usually arrives when the sky is clear and the ground is not protected by clouds. The ground can easily lack that protection when there is no moon, in which case those who believe in folklore don't count that one.

Last week the thermometer dropped into the high thirties and I began to eye my vegetables with some concern. I rushed out to the garden each morning to determine if those unfailing thermometers, the squash vines, had wilted, and each morning, finding them unblackened, I held my breath for another night. The full moon came in a night of cloudless glory, and the full moon passed, and still the squash remained unscathed. Then, one windy blue morning, I heard on the weather report that a high was moving in from Canada (frost is always blamed on our northern neighbors), and I figured I had pushed my luck far enough. All that day we plundered the garden and by evening the barn floor, the greenhouse, the shed floor, and any other place where there was space was piled high with the fruits of our summer's labor. Squash, melons, tomatoes, peppers, eggplant, onions, carrots, turnips, and beets lay strewn in glorious abandon. I was a pioneer. I was a self-supporting man of the soil. I had a head as big as one of my cabbages—and then my wife asked, "What are we going to do with all of this stuff?"

Not the smallest problem of the successful amateur gardener is how to store the results of his season's work. Most, of course, will not have as much to take care of as we have, but all things are relative and the man with a smaller garden is apt to live in a smaller house. He is not apt to own a barn or a cold cellar, and his refrigerator space may be less. We have, however, a common solution, which is to pick out the best of the crop and the part we can most easily store, and throw the rest on the compost heap.

The most convenient way to preserve food (or most of it) is by freezing, but it is not the only way. It is hard for the young to believe, but it is true, that mechanical refrigerators did not come into general domestic use until the late 1930s. That is, of course, a long time ago if you are only thirty-five, and is coeval with the discovery of America if you are only twenty; but believe it or not there are a lot of citizens, not yet senile, who recall with clarity and some affection the old icebox. Iceboxes kept food very well. They did not dehydrate it, as do electrical refrigerators, but neither did they provide the convenience of "deep freezing." However, long before there was mechanical refrigeration, people stored food over winter by canning. True, freezing is simpler and, in some cases, the food tastes better, but with very little extra effort many vegetables may be packed in glass for winter use and there is nothing much more satisfying than the sight of a long shelf of jars filled with tomatoes, and beets, and jams and jellies and other goodies to warm the heart and stomach on a snowy winter day.

If you have friends or neighbors you can offer some of your abundance to them but, if your experience is like mine, you will find that most of those who admired your garden in the summer are reluctant to take any of the produce in the fall, particularly if it involves any work on their part. The truth is that people generally, even country dwellers, have grown so accustomed to opening a can, or a package of frozen food, that the idea of lugging

home a dirty old bunch of beets or turnips, or a peck of unshelled peas, and starting from scratch seems unnatural. It is unfortunate that this is so, and it is not the smallest reason the cost of food is so high. A pea is a pea is a pea, but by the time it has been shelled and washed and graded and mixed with butter and placed in a boil-proof plastic container, and packed in a pretty box embellished with a color picture depicting the contents all green and buttery, the spoonful of peas costs four times as much as the fresh product. Don't blame the farmer; he gets no more, and don't blame the processor too much. Just blame yourself for buying convenience instead of food. If you have none of your own, the way to buy frozen peas is in a five-pound bag from which you can shake out the few you need for a meal and do all the buttering and baloney yourself.

If you can manage to find a place in your house where the temperature stays below fifty degrees but does not freeze, you can store a great many vegetables dry. Onions, including shallots (the best keepers of all), and winter squash, do very well spread on an attic floor in the dark. Look them over occasionally and discard any that show signs of decay. Beets and carrots and yellow turnips keep a long time in cartons filled with peat moss or sawdust; they won't last all winter but if you can keep them through Christmas you are that much ahead of the game. Potatoes do quite well in an ordinary sack under similar conditions if you rub the sprouts off every few weeks and keep them in the dark. If you are lucky enough to have a dirt-floored cellar you have it made, for the damper air prevents shriveling, but you still have to keep your eye on things. Remember the old adage about the rotten apple.

I have said nothing about dried beans because everyone knows how to keep them, but I would guess that not many today remember that not so long ago, peas were grown to be dried and not very many were consumed green. Eating fresh green peas was a luxury that one did not indulge in very often; the reason for growing them was to keep one alive in winter. Peas can still be dried if you lack freezer space, and what is better on a frosty winter day than a bowl of steaming dried pea soup with a few scraps of crisp salt pork floating around on the surface?

Central Heat

Happy, one of the Brittany spaniels who blesses us with her affection, came into my room early this morning. The clock had just struck two when she jumped onto my bed and snuggled up into my back. She likes the cozy feeling of the fuzzy coverlet I sleep under. She is no problem, for once she is settled, she keeps very still. When, in an hour or so, she decided to go and to favor my wife with her company, she left with a minimum of disturbance. I have never been able to determine what it is that causes her to leave, but she must have some reasons of her own that are incomprehensible to a merely human mind.

I suppose there are people who would be violently opposed to having a dog share their bed with them. If that is the way they feel about it I am sure it is not for me to attempt to change their minds, though I must say that during a couple of wars and a decade at sea, I have had far less desirable bedfellows. But there, others may have led more sheltered lives or, perhaps, they belong to that narcissistic club that believes *Homo sapiens* to be a superior species, a conclusion that history (both past and currently in the making) would suggest is debatable.

After Happy left me, I lay there luxuriating in the comfort of a warm bed in a cold room, although the small of my back was not as warm as it had been prior to losing my bedfellow. I was comfortable though, and having nothing specific to worry about lay quietly conversing with my mind. There is a difference between that and worrying. Being a light sleeper, I have always spent some part of the dark hours in wakefulness and, when I was young, devoted it to worrying. The middle of the night seems eminently suited to this activity. There is nothing else going on to distract one's thoughts, so eventually they run in the same line for long enough that they wear down a track you can't see out of. But, as I said, I was not worrying. One of the many advantages of growing old is that, unlike being young, you don't have so many years ahead to concern yourself with. When you are twenty you have (if I recall American mortality tables more or less accurately) about fifty-five years—that is, until you are seventy-five. I do not. I can spit, from where I am, over the eighty-year line. Backward, that is. I am pretty sure, barring politicians and nuclear bombs, of what is going to happen to the world I am going to live in.

I was thinking as I lay there what comfortable sounds old houses make. On bitterly cold nights they creak and groan as ships do when they are rolling easily in a seaway. The heating pipes in the walls echo with a series of small knocks as they expand and rub against the studs or floor joists.

Every time the furnace ignites there is a rumble and then a steady, sustained gentle roar, until the thermostat turns it off again. The windows rattle, and so do the shutters.

Going to bed is a very simple matter these days. You put out the cat, turn down the thermostat, brush your teeth, switch off the lights, and there you are. When I was younger (not centuries ago) America did not worry about Arab oil. Some gasoline was refined, but most of the crude oil went into kerosene that provided oil for the lamps of China. China, Maine, as well as China, the world. Houses, other than those heated with wood, were kept warm by coal-fired furnaces that provided the steam that made the radiators crackle. There was no switching off of lights and turning down of thermostats. You turned the flame in the Aladdin as low as you could, cupped your hand around the top of the chimney, and gave a gentle puff. The furnace was a little more time consuming. Before going to bed the fireman-designate went down cellar and banked the furnace for the night, which involved exactly the right proportions of coal and ashes, and a delicate adjustment of the draft. If he was good at it, all it took in the morning to get up a head of steam was to shake the grate bars, break up the surface of the coals and skillfully spread a shovelful of "buckwheat" across it and open the drafts. If he was not, the fire that remained would be anywhere between moribund and dead. A catastrophe of cataclysmic immensity on a zero morning.

As I lay there in my bed listening to the quiet functioning of twentieth century automated equipment, I realized that the delicate rasping of snow against glass, which had lulled me to sleep a few hours before, had ceased and that, even though the draperies were drawn, the room was light enough to distinguish objects plainly. I thought to myself, "I am so comfortable, but I *must* get up and look out at the moon," so I clutched my bathrobe about me, went to the window, and drew back the draperies. Moonlight flooded over me and I looked out on a night filled with splendor. An enormous moon lit the bare, white, snow-covered field and accentuated the blackness of the surrounding woods. I stood entranced. All was motionless as a charcoal drawing, as still as death, but with that eerie luminescence of moonlight on snow, I felt that I was witnessing a moment of creation: the world cold, bare, and uninhabited, as it once was and will someday be again.

As I stood there a small, cold, wet nose slipped into my hand to remind me of my warm bed. I hurried back, and in a moment that gentle nudging below my shoulder blades reminded me that I had not been alone in my vigil.

Winter Neighbors

Every year after town meeting I begin to kid myself that spring is at hand but I should know, by now, that March in Maine is for the most part solid winter. The snow may go off, here and there on the south sides of boulders and buildings, and an adventurous snowdrop show its head, but a day later there can be another foot of that white stuff. I suppose, though, I should not complain, for it is a good snow cover that brings plants through the winter unharmed. Nevertheless I long to see the ground again.

The temperature has been in the forties for the last two days but it was there last week also, which deceived me into thinking we were in for a March thaw, but not so. We had another northeaster that put us right back where we started. Hope, however, springs eternal, particularly in the breasts of gardeners, so I ventured forth this morning without my snowshoes and did not sink into the drifts more than six inches.

All my better shrubs were browsed back to stubs by deer a winter ago, so I covered everything with netting last fall. We have a large garden and I used more netting than I could justify, but it is bitter to see the growth of years disappear in a few weeks. I have, anyhow, the satisfaction of knowing that my extravagance paid off because, except for a few odd twigs, everything came through uncropped.

There are not as many deer tracks around as there were last year, which I lay to the fact that the free lunch counter has been discontinued. Other tracks there are aplenty. The snowshoe rabbits (hares really) never seem to venture far from cover. You will see the elongated tracks they make emerging from under a spruce tree and then following the edge of the woodland until they again disappear. Mice and chipmunks keep close to stone walls and emergency funk holes in the snow. I read somewhere that chipmunks hibernate, which may very well be true in some places, but they do not do so around here. Our yellow cat, Butterscotch, keeps his hand in all winter by practicing on chipmunks. Out front we have a rough stone wall that is not much more than a long pile of rocks. They were dug out or dragged off the place when the house was built 125 years ago. It is high enough to escape being completely overwhelmed by all but the most horrendous blizzards, so it is a chipmunk haven. Almost any sunny day during the winter a chippie can be seen sitting on the wall twitching its tail, and almost any day Butterscotch will be seen trying to sneak up on it. In summer he slays them by the dozen but they rarely appear on his menu in winter. I lay this to his dislike of deep snow and the fact that he does not get enough exercise to work off the enormous amounts of Kitty Salmon that Mom stuffs into him. Now, if I could only teach Butterscotch to murder deer with the skill and enthusiasm he does mice, birds, and chipmunks, I'd buy him a hunting license. The fact that he would hunt out of season would merely confirm his Maine birthright.

The chippies have other enemies too. I saw a weasel track headed straight for the wall. Weasels don't fool around. When they are hunting they keep their eyes on their prey and, if you are in the way, will run right over your foot to get to their objective. In winter they are almost invisible. They are solid white, but for the tip of the tail, which is black. I found a weasel last year in a closet drawer in our guest house. I don't know how it got there but it had, obviously, been unable to escape. It was desiccated and stiff but apart from that and the glaze over its eyes it seemed alive. It would have made a good companion for an embalmed pharaoh.

I was given a thistle-feeder for Christmas. This is not a device to feed thistles. They do not need feeding; they live on adversity and generate their kind by immaculate conception—or so it seems. The thistle-feeder that Santa Claus brought me is a nylon net tube about a foot long and two inches in diameter. The idea is to fill it with thistle seed and hang it in a tree to feed goldfinches. After a few false starts, when the seed ran straight through the holes onto the kitchen floor, I mastered the art and got it filled and hung in a tree. An hour later it was empty. It had been banging on a branch and the seed was all on the ground. Next time I hung it in the clear but it only lasted a day after the goldfinches found it. With thistle seed at sixty cents a pound I don't know if I shall make it through the winter—perhaps I can arrange for a small loan at the bank. I have always liked goldfinches, and my affection for them has increased since they have demonstrated how much thistle seed they can consume. But I can't help wondering if I am not just tolling them in for Butterscotch to add to his Kitty Salmon—I just saw him lurking around a corner with the tip of his tail moving ever so slowly from side to side.

Four-footed Friends

For the first time since we bought the old Bowden place, twenty years ago, there are no animals in the barn. Oh, there are a couple of dozen chickens, if you want to consider them as animals, but there are none with four feet. We have our dogs, of course, but they are about two-thirds human and they don't live in the barn. The little one, Gay, sleeps on the foot of my wife's bed and Happy sleeps on mine. I was told, in Mexico, that the Aztecs kept dogs as bedfellows to keep them comfortable on bitter nights on the *alto plano* at 9,000 feet. They ate them too, which I could no more do than practice cannibalism but, I guess, it is all in the way one is brought up.

The reason the barn is bereft of quadrupeds is that I am grown too old to look after them. I have never done it entirely alone, anyway, but I have always done my share. I am not ailing or feeble and have no more than my appropriate allotment of the disabilities that people my age are entitled to, but chasing a bull along the highway, or pitching hay down from the mow, or wrestling old ewes, is not, I have discovered, something you do to cure angina pectoris. Not unless you want to cure it permanently and abruptly.

My neighbor, Andy, told me there was no point in having animals unless you could care for them yourself, and that was why he had gotten rid of his—and he is quite correct. My eighteenth-century ancestors may have been satisfied to have some lesser mortals look after a herd of cattle or flock of sheep on the far side of a ha-ha for landscape effect, but I enjoy more intimate contact. Frankly, I like the smell of a barn; and shoveling out cow dung or horse manure I do not find distasteful. I might if I had had fifty milkers to muck out twice a day, but the residue from two or three animals is nothing, and I am able to keep in mind what it is going to do for my garden. What it does is magnificent.

I have a feeling that at least a portion of our problems today arise from the fact that most of us have been torn up by the roots from the land where for so many generations we lived in close relationship with animals. We find ourselves alone, without the unavoidable daily responsibilities that rural life imposes. Only a couple of generations ago most of us lived on farms or in small towns where we were part of an interlocking society. Through the necessity of performing a task ourselves we could see the result, and we accepted without question the notion that society could only function as a whole by others doing the same thing. The farm families depended upon each other. If anyone was ill or away or died, the rest had to reapportion the work or seek the help of a neighbor. The shopkeeper or shoemaker, baker or carpenter, or other tradesman in a small town, had visibly laid out before him the reciprocal nature of society. We have dispersed so far from prime causes in these latter days that we have forgotten that it is not an omnipotent computer that is the provider, but a lot of other men and women like ourselves doing individual tasks. If the airplane is not on time or the lights go out or the road is not plowed and sanded some snowy morning, we blame it on the airline or the utility or the Highway Department. Actually, Pan American never flew a mile or sold a ticket; the Bangor Hydro Electric Company never climbed a light pole in the middle of an ice storm. If the help dropped dead, the Highway Department couldn't roll a truck. A corporation or a government is an entity that has neither body nor soul.

One of the reasons I came back to the country after living at home and abroad in urban surroundings for half my life was because I wanted to regain my brotherhood with, and appreciation of, my fellow men and women. I wanted to live again where I could see what made things work. I wanted to be a part of the action.

That I have succeeded is obvious to me and I feel that my dumb animals (as the Victorians called them) have been a major contributing factor. You cannot run a farm, even a farm that never makes a profit in dollars, without being rewarded in what is sometimes called psychic income. Who knows what *real* income is anyway? Going into my barn on a cold winter night to make sure that the cattle have water and feed and bedding, and to be greeted by them, is reward enough. I don't know how many people, except farmers, know it—but cows have a unique way of saying "hello." I hope it does not sound vulgar to refined city ears but, as any dairy farmer knows, a cow (a family cow anyway) will invariably drop a flop when you go into the tie-up. Not very elegant, perhaps, but an acknowledgment of your presence, and who said life was elegant? A woman giving birth is not elegant either, but if it did not happen with considerable frequency we would not be here.

One can learn affection from animals, too. I know of few things more touching than the way of a cow with a calf. After it is born the mother cleans it up and nudges it to its feet to nurse. It is helplessness personified. Its legs are too long and its body too heavy. It tries to stand and staggers and falls down. It does it not once but many times. Each time the cow reaches down to it and murmurs mother-talk, and if you have never heard 1,000 pounds of cow crooning to a newborn calf, you have no idea how closely we are related.

I shall miss my four-footed friends but, who knows? Perhaps I can talk someone into lending me a couple of cows or sheep in the summer. They can keep my pasture mowed and there will be enough grass for them during the warm weather. They will be insurance, too, that the swallows I have opened the haymow window for these many years will not pass me by when they come north again.

Books

Amongst my other vices, which are numerous, I have, all my life, been a collector of books and at last count owned 3,000 or 4,000. Having long since outgrown available shelf space, they are now beginning to pile up on the floor under the dining room sideboard.

Except for dictionaries, encyclopedias, and the like, I have read all I own, some several times, but I still am unable to resist the temptation of buying more. Ecclesiastes records, "Of making many books there is no end; and much study is a weariness of the flesh." While I agree with the first statement I cannot agree with the conclusion, much as it pains me to quarrel with Holy Writ.

I read somewhere recently that there have been more books published since 1950 than in the previous 500 years—that is, since Gutenberg printed the Mazarin Bible in 1456. I can well believe this but except for a miniscule number they are unlikely to add to my storage problem. Most of them are technical works beyond my comprehension or interest, and an untold quantity of the remainder would have better rested hidden in the wombs of their authors. It is unfortunate that no one has devised a contraceptive to be administered to writers. Only on the rarest of occasions do I buy a book less than five years old; I would guess that the vast majority of books in my library were published at least twenty-five years ago and a goodly number are more than a century old.

Novels roll off the presses in untold millions and a few of them do manage to wash up on these shores. I rarely buy any, but our summer guests do and leave them when they go, along with an odd sneaker, a half a jar of marmalade, an empty can that once contained black fly repellent, and odd copies of *Playboy* and *Penthouse*. These body-beautiful magazines have diminished in number since my grandson married. Not even the centerfold playmate of the month, with her dimensional perfection, can stand up to the real thing.

When I came to live in Maine it was not long before I discovered that the only way I would have any time to myself would be by taking steps to keep house guests under control. I did so by making a second library out of our first floor bedroom so that my wife and I would occupy the only other sleeping quarters. I then converted an old store that had been in front of the barn into a guest house. I can now tell my guests, as the English do, "I'll see you for a drink at 6:30—go off and enjoy yourselves." In addition to solving the visitor problem, the guest house also provides a convenient place to get rid of paperbacks and other volumes I once felt I should read but did not want to keep. I could have thrown them away but, as any booklover knows, to discard even the most worthless book is a traumatic experience.

I said to Helen this morning, "Let's go to England this summer." She agreed, for she knows and likes England as much as I do, but questioned, "Any particular reason?" I replied that one did not really need a reason but that I thought it might be fun to get a little car and wander around looking in old bookshops and buying a few odd volumes here and there. Being an understanding wife she did not say, "My God, where are you going to put them?" But rather, "Where did you get that idea?" I responded by telling her I had been reading the most recent number of *In Britain,* where there was an article on antiquarian bookstores. I went on to inform her that I had learned there was, in Hay-on-Wye (a quiet and pretty town on the Welsh border) the largest antiquarian bookstore in the world. The establishment, run by a youngish man named Richard Booth, stocks more than a million volumes. They are housed in an abandoned movie theatre, Hay Castle, Cockcroft House, and half a dozen other buildings about town.

Helen and I know the southern Marches, as that part of the country is called, quite well, as we stayed in a pub, the Baskerville Arms (in Clyro) some years ago when we were immersing ourselves in the ambience of a notable clerical diarist of the nineteenth century named Reverend Francis Kilvert. Hay-on-Wye is nearby and would be a good place to begin a book-buyer's pilgrimage. Prices in London and the tourist centers are out of sight, but you can still get a pretty good room and breakfast in the country without bankrupting yourself. You may have to walk over a few yards of cold linoleum to get to the "john," which translates "loo" in England, but that won't kill you. *En passant,* I have always wondered why that necessary establishment is masculine in the United States and feminine in England.

The foregoing brings me to the genesis of this piece. I received a book from London the other day called *Southey's Tour in the Netherlands.* It was published posthumously in 1902, just about the time I learned to read, and describes a trip Southey made to the battlefield of Waterloo in 1815. Southey's description of Waterloo is a chilling education but my interest, as a gardener, was attracted to a passing observation he made on October 20:

> *Five leagues to Brussels . . . Edith May's quick eyes discovered the small or lilliput cabbages growing like warts upon the stalks of what seemed common cabbages; and no doubt they are an artificial product.*

If, in 1815, Southey did not recognize Brussels sprouts there cannot have been many in England, which is a surprise to me, for it is an agile man indeed who, in the twentieth century, is able to avoid eating the ubiquitous sprout at least once a day while he is in that country.

I have never been an all-out admirer of Southey's poetry but I am encouraged to return to it after reading the journal of his tour. I am afraid, though, he was a selfish young man as he dragged his sister along on the journey so he would have company, even though she was ill and had to leave behind four young children. I will allow him to speak for himself:

> *She had left home in ill health and worse spirits; both worsened during the long journey from Keswick to Ramsgate; and the best hope I now had was that seasickness, with the total and frequent change of air, scene, and circumstance, would remove what began to appear a very formidable malady.*

All I can add is that seasickness appears to me to be a rather harsh remedy for any illness.

The book was published in Boston by Houghton Mifflin in a limited edition of 519 copies and is a delight of the bookmaker's art. That I found it in England is an added excuse for haunting antiquarian bookshops wherever one may find them.

Pardon the Past—Give Grace for the Future

In a sheltered corner of my garden grows a modest little rose named Omar Khayyam. It is reputed to have been propagated from a Damask rose growing on Edward FitzGerald's grave at Boulge, Suffolk, which was planted there in 1893 as a seedling from a rose on Omar Khayyam's grave at Naishapur. It is not the rose that Omar sang about when he wrote "I sometimes think that never blows so red / The Rose as where some buried Caesar bled," for it is pink, not red. I cherish it because I have always loved the *Rubaiyat* and, in my youth, could recite the entire poem by heart. Even now some quatrains remain with me and, glancing at the calendar this morning and noting that it was but a few days until the new year, I was reminded: "Now the New Year reviving old Desires, / The thoughtful Soul to Solitude retires."

I retired a good many years ago or, more correctly, moved to the country, but I did not make the mistake of many who retire: that is, cut myself adrift from life and expect to find paradise in idleness. Charles Lamb, probably the greatest of all English essayists, was so overjoyed when he was able to retire from the East India Company that he wrote one of his most famous pieces, "The Superannuated Man." In it he gave a definition of retirement. He wrote: "I walk about, not to and from," which would certainly suit those thousands who hurry to places of employment in the morning and reverse the procedure at night. After Lamb's retirement he had more time to devote to his writing, so he was not idle either, and it is by his essays that we remember him, not by his job with the East India Company.

I have done fairly well as regards solitude. I am not a hermit and am seldom completely alone, for I have a loving wife and friendly neighbors; but the only dwelling I can see from where I live is a lighthouse and its service buildings. There are a few more houses along our road that leads a mile-and-a-half to Naskeag Harbor but I cannot see them for the trees, and around here we believe in Robert Frost's dictum that "Good fences make good neighbors," and tend to our own business.

I have kept a diary most of my life and sometimes refer to it to see what changes, if any, have occurred in my viewpoint. I have long held the opinion that none of us change direction, that there are not many Saul-on-the-road-to-Damascus conversions, and that in old age we are usually as we were when we were young, only more so. The difference is in intensity, not direction. I find this confirmed in a diary entry for January first, 1945. I had been reflecting on the occurrences of a rainy day nearly thirty years before *that* date—which was a long time previous. It had been a day of small bread but the incidents remained clearly in my mind. I recited them and then added:

> *It is strange how life is made up of small recollections. Memory, it seems, often does not consider worth filing for future reference things we consider of vast importance. Instead, it selects experiences like these as if to point out to us how unimportant are most of the day-to-day concerns we labor so heavily over.*

I have not changed my mind about this.

Later that year, On August seventh, the day after the explosion of the atom bomb in Hiroshima, I find I was shocked, as were millions of others, at the possibilities of disaster inherent in "the bomb." I mourned the death and maiming of the thousands of Japanese in Hiroshima, and wrote:

The times are out of joint. We can read in the paper or hear on the radio of vast undertakings and stupendous events ten minutes after they occur, but our neighbor separated from us by a two-inch plaster wall can die in lonely misery and we may never know it. What kind of a world is this? I would like to live in the deep country and know a few people well and work with my hands and fill my soul with the small things, the tangible understandable things, of life. The chorus of birds at dawn on a fresh spring morning. The hot, fragrant smell of baking from the kitchen. The clatter of the mower in the field. Rich yellow cream in an old blue pitcher. My wife's head on my shoulder on a cold winter night with the stars shining frostily through the window. What meaning has $100 billion, 700 million board feet of lumber, a bomb with the power to obliterate a city, or a population of 800 million Chinese? None, to me. I am a little man, just one man; my lumber is what I buy from Jake's Yard to mend my garage. My Chinaman is old Ah Fong who has three whiskers on each side of his chin and irons my Sunday shirts. And I am convinced that the world is made up of other little men who ask only to be left in peace, and want no more of their governments than that they should do those things that can be better done collectively than individually. I doubt they want grandiose planning or to be led into a new millennium. I believe they would be willing to concede their more vociferous neighbor a little more than his share, in preference to fighting about it, knowing well enough that in the fullness of time the balance will come even again.

Thus I wrote thirty-two years ago. I do live in the country and I haven't changed very much, and neither has the world, and I doubt we shall. I give you old Omar's plaint but without much hope that anyone will ever achieve what he visualized:

> *Ah Love! could you and I with Him conspire*
> *To grasp this sorry Scheme of Things entire,*
> *Would we not shatter it to bits—and then*
> *Re-mould it nearer to the Heart's Desire!*

I am not sure of what I shall be thinking on the first day of January, but I have a good idea. If of nothing else, I shall be pondering upon how fortunate I am to have lived this past year in peace and goodwill among friendly neighbors in the quiet and tranquility of rural surroundings. Few men in these days are so blessed.

New Year's Day is a time when we stop and take stock, if we ever do, of our blessings. We think too of our failures, of our accomplishments, and of our goals. Some of us make resolutions about our future conduct which we only rarely keep. Why we choose New Year's Day rather than some other day for these trials of will, particularly if we live in the country, is not clear. For the countryman every day is the day of a new year, for there is not any starting or stopping or beginning or ending to nature.

I suppose for the purely mechanical necessities of constructing a calendar, the day that we call New Year's Day is as good as any other, although one would think that the spring solstice would have been more appropriate. All it does is mark a watershed between the past and the future, but the date is an arbitrary election and is observed at different times by different cultures.

I am reminded of a remark made by Christopher Morley while crossing the Atlantic Ocean. He said that somewhere in that wide sea there must be a spot where the waters divide, back to back, for they surge onto the shores of Europe and America with equal insistence. Although I am hazy about the theory of relativity I think that Albert Einstein concluded that time was something like that. He theorized that there was neither beginning nor end, that there was an amalgam of time and space, and that "time is private to each body."

We all have our private new year, when we make resolutions, and rarely does it coincide with the Gregorian calendar. It comes when the hounds of past sins are hot upon our traces. We make our resolutions to quiet our consciences, as men take baking soda to quiet their stomachs, and with as little permanent effect.

I thought I would see what Henry Thoreau had to say about new year's resolutions, but although I spent all one afternoon reading in his journals when I should have been working, I discovered only silence on New Year's Day. When I consulted the index I found him thinking of new year's resolutions in the spring. On March 31, 1852 he wrote:

Perchance as we grow old we cease to spring with the spring, and we are indifferent to the succession of years, and they go by without epochs as months. Woe be to us when we cease to form new resolutions on the opening of a new year.

I am afraid I cannot agree. I have lived to be older than Henry was when he died and believe that had he lived longer he, too, might have thought differently. We countrymen, even when we grow old, still spring with the spring, and if we no longer make new year's resolutions it is not because we are unmindful of our shortcomings, but rather because time has taught us that it takes more than resolutions to gather figs from thistles.

Time flows on for all of us regardless of how we choose to measure it; the best we can do is to stand quietly, not wearying the gods with our promises of future virtue, and listen to the rustle of its passing.

Here are the words of a kindly and thoughtful man, the Reverend Francis Kilvert, penned more than a century ago on December 31, 1871:

> *And here is the end of another year. How much to be thankful for. How much to be mourned over. God pardon the past and give grace for the future, and make the New Year better than the old.*

Roy Barrette was born in America but grew up in England, then went to sea for ten years before beginning a long and successful business career in Philadelphia. Since 1962 he and his wife have lived on their farm in the little coastal settlement of Brooklin, Maine, where he writes a weekly column on rural life that appears in the Ellsworth, Maine, *American* and the Pittsfield, Massachusetts, *Berkshire Eagle*. In three recent years the Maine Press Association has named the column the best in its class.

Richard Gorski, who illustrated *A Countryman's Journal,* is a former New Yorker who now lives with his family in an 1840 farmhouse in the same town as the author, where he is associate art director of *WoodenBoat* magazine.